Painting
Toads & Turtles
in
Gouache

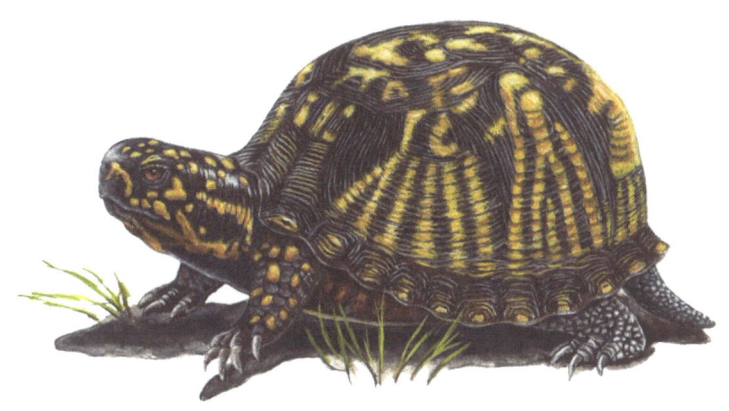

Written and Illustrated
by
Sandy Williams

Index

Introduction

We've been depicting animals in our art since prehistoric times. Bison and deer dance across the cave walls in Lascaux. Cats, horses and birds bejewel the walls of Egyptian homes and tombs. The paintings of Landseer in the 19th century are embedded in the English culture. And our fascination with animal art continues today.

I've always loved painting animals, all kinds, and I ultimately settled on gouache as my main medium because I can capture every little detail of fur and flashing eyes. I hope I can guide you and inspire you to paint the creatures we see around us.

In this class I demonstrate how to use gouache to paint two very different types of reptiles: an American Toad and an Eastern Box Turtle. You'll learn a lot about gouache techniques as you work on these two exercises, along with a separate blending exercise using a simple snail image.

Please note that for the purposes of clear demonstrations I've broken the toad and turtle down into sections so that we concentrate on one part of the subject at a time. In the real world you probably wouldn't work like this, although, at times, I've finished the head of an animal before I began the body. When you begin your own paintings, experiment and find out what works best for you. You may approach each animal differently. There is no rule that says you have to do every painting the same way every time, or that you have to finish one section before another.

I hope you enjoy exploring gouache and all it can do to help you paint realistic animals!

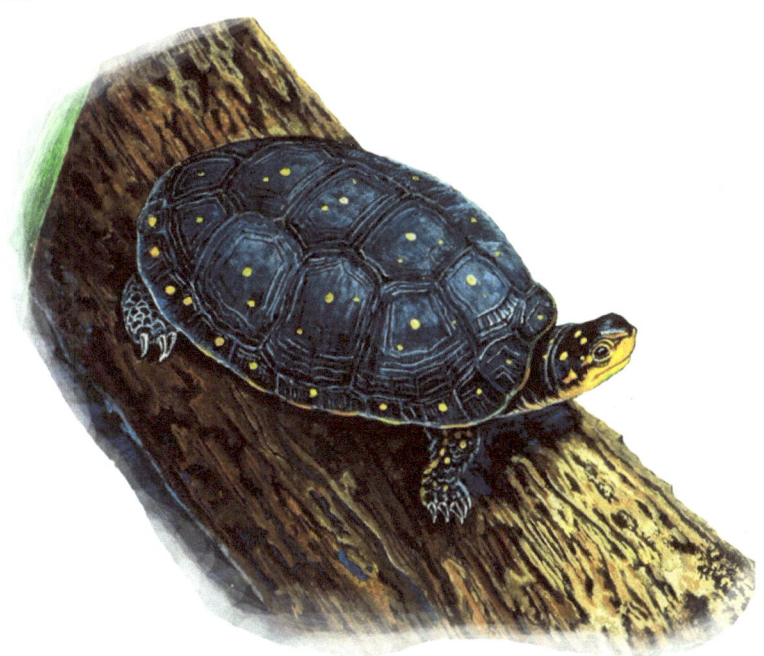

Gouache

Gouache is an opaque watercolor. The pigments are bound by a liquid glue, like Gum Arabic, and white pigment or chalk is added for more opacity. It has an almost suede like finish and lines painted with gouache can be very sharp. The colors can be brilliant or very subtle. It has a centuries old history and has been used for anything from illuminated manuscripts to modern commercial advertising work.

There are many brands of gouache available. I use mostly Winsor & Newton because it's easy to find and of good quality. Other brands are M. Graham, Holbein, Schmincke and Daler Rowney.

The first time you use gouache squeeze a small amount of color onto your palette. Even though you don't use it all up right away you'll be able to reconstitute it with water for later use. The only time this won't work is when you have a large area to cover. Use fresh paint for that or you'll get little lumps of undisolved paint in yur piece. If that happens brush them off and touch up.

Don't add a lot of water to the paint, or fill up the paint well on your palette with water. Water is added to the paint a little at a time by dipping your brush in water and then working it into one side of your spot of paint. The paint should have a creamy consistency. If you add too much water the paint will lose its opacity. One exception in these exercises is when we paint an underpainting. In this instance we use a thinner layer of paint to cover the white of the paper before painting the top layers. The colors can be mixed in another well on the palette or, sometimes, directly on the painting.

One of the great advantages of gouache is that it's very "forgiving." If you find that a certain area is not working just paint over it and start again.

Start by squeezing out spots of paint about this size

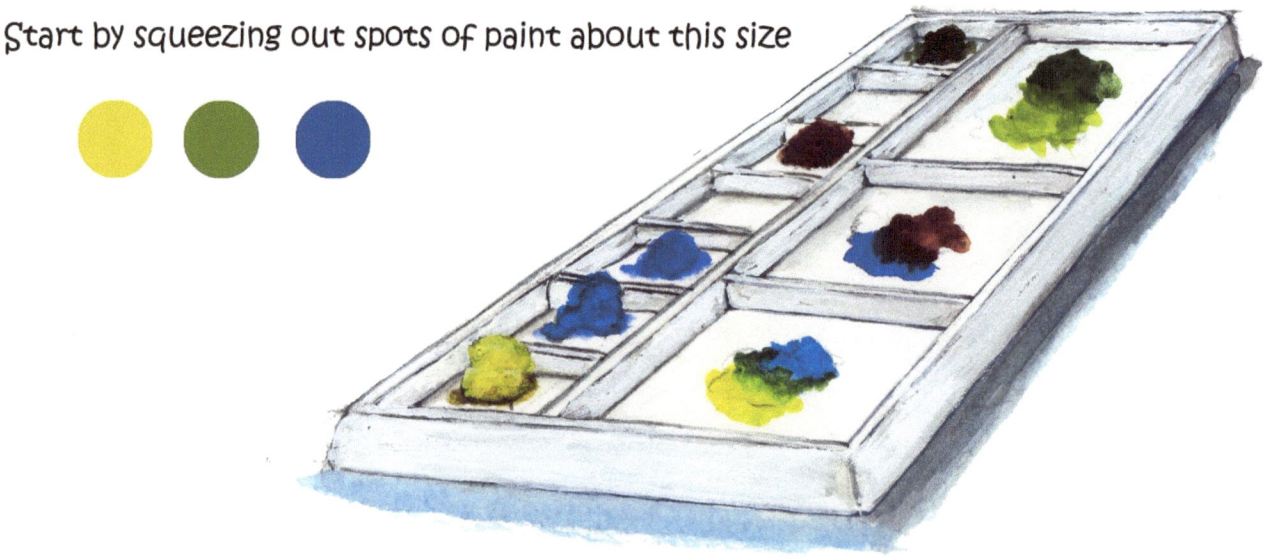

Materials List

PENCILS -- I generally use a softer pencil, like a 4B, to draw with but use whatever you're comfortable with. Just make sure that you don't make your marks so hard that they're hard to erase. I use a kneaded eraser because it won't leave little crumbly bits of material that have to be brushed off.

PAPER -- I recommend using hot press watercolor paper, preferably 140 #, although a little lighter weight would be OK, too. Some artists use illustration board, vellum or bristol.   I use Arches 140# hot press because it has a nice, smooth surface to make detailing easier and crisper looking. Experiment and try some different papers. One quarter standard size sheet should be plenty for this course.

PALETTE -- It should be white so you can see exactly what color you're mixing. If you don't have a palette a white paper plate works fine. It's just a little harder to transport wet paint if you have to move around.

WATER CONTAINER -- Use whatever you have on hand. At home I use 5 ounce disposable Dixie cups or used (and washed) plastic cat food containers.

TRANSFER PAPER -- Depending on how you transfer your images you may or may not need some plain tracing paper. An 11" x 14" sheet folded in half should do.

BRUSHES -- You'll probably need three small watercolor brushes: a 4/0 small round, a #1 small round and an 18/0 liner brush

GOUACHE -- The seven tubes listed here will give you enough variety of colors to complete all the illustrations in this course. The brand I use is Winsor & Newton but that's not a requirement.

Permanent White
Olive Green
Burnt Umber
Burnt Sienna

Primary Red
Brilliant Yellow
Ultramarine Blue

Before You Begin

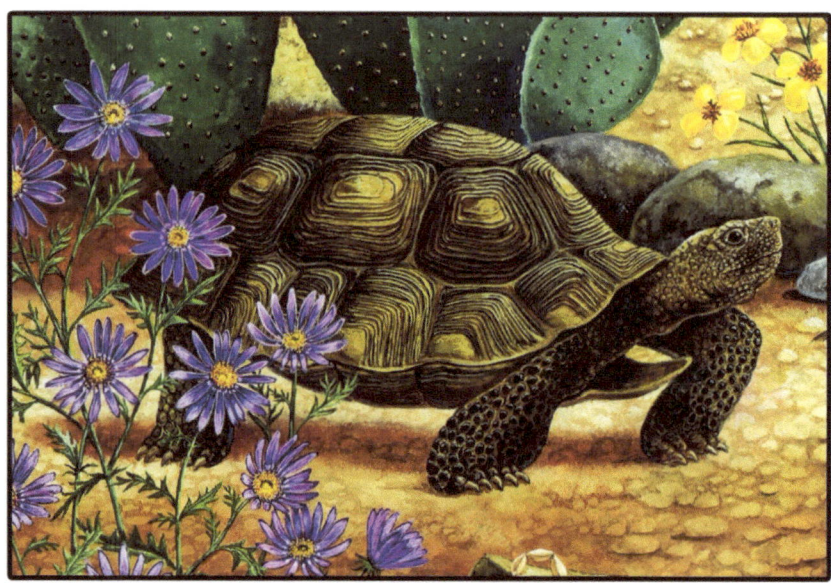

Here are a few tips on health and safety.

BE AWARE! Some of the pigments we work with are poisonous. Visit a site like http://www.ci.tucson.az.us/arthazards for specific information on the pigments or processes you use.

For this course please remember three things.

1. Don't put the tips of your brushes in your mouth!

2. Wash your hands after painting before you eat.

3. Get up and stretch frequently. Besides loosening up your body you'll come back to your painting with fresh eyes and it will be easier to see the progress you've made and what has yet to be done.

Colors and Values

A few notes on color:

Color is fleeting, fugitive and ever changing. Colors of animals can change with the type of light, the time of day, reflections from grass, sky, buildings, water, the age of the animal or the time of year. Some animals naturally have different colors in the same species. The American Toad, for instance, can range from gray to reddish brown. So don't stress out if you don't get the color you want "exactly right." In this class you'll be using a limited palette of only seven tubes of gouache, but you'll still be able to realistically depict the reptiles.

Values:

What you really need to be careful about is value. Value is the lightness or darkness of your paint, and without a good range of values your painting will look a bit boring, without, well . . . sparkle! Some samples of the value scales you'll be using are below.

We won't be using black in this class, but please note how dark the Burnt Umber and Ultramarine Blue mixture can be and how it compares to black.

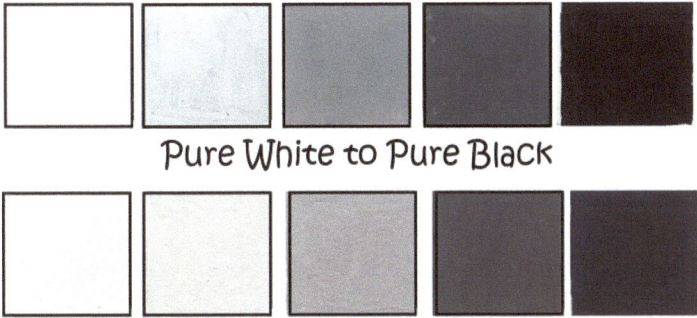

Pure White to Pure Black

Burnt Umber/Ultramarine Blue: light to dark

Getting Started

The following three demonstrations show how to use gouache to paint an American Toad, an Eastern Box Turtle and a simple snail. Look at each step carefully and read the descriptions. Sometimes you'll be dealing with very small changes that make very big differences in the finished painting. These demonstrations are only guidelines. Feel free to explore the possibilites. Remember, gouache is a very forgiving medium. If you try something and it doesn't seem to be working, you can always paint over it and start again.

At the beginning of each section is a page with a black and white line drawing of the painting. Use this page to transfer the image to your piece of 140# hot press watercolor paper. There are many ways to transfer images. Using a light box is one way, but holding the page up to a window that has sun streaming through it and then putting your watercolor paper over it to trace works just as well. Or, you could put soft graphite (from a soft pencil) on the back of the transfer page, put it directly on top of your watercolor paper and then trace over the lines so they are transferred to your paper that way. I usually keep a piece of tracing paper handy and cover it completely with soft graphite. Then, when I need to transfer an image, I slip it on top of my watercolor paper, graphite side down, and put the page that has the image on it on top. Then I trace the lines to transfer the image. I've used the same piece of tracing paper for over ten years. I just add more graphite to it with a soft 6B pencil when the images get too light. When not in use I keep it folded in half so it doesn't smear all over everything around it.

So. . . get started and enjoy this versatile medium!

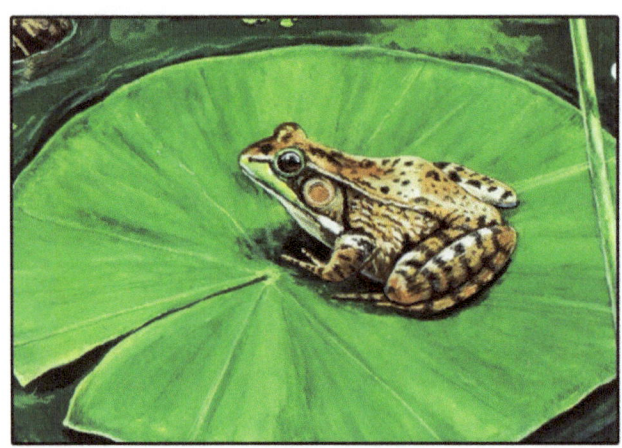

Simple Snail Blending Exercise

Colors Used: Permanent White, Burnt Umber, Ultramarine Blue

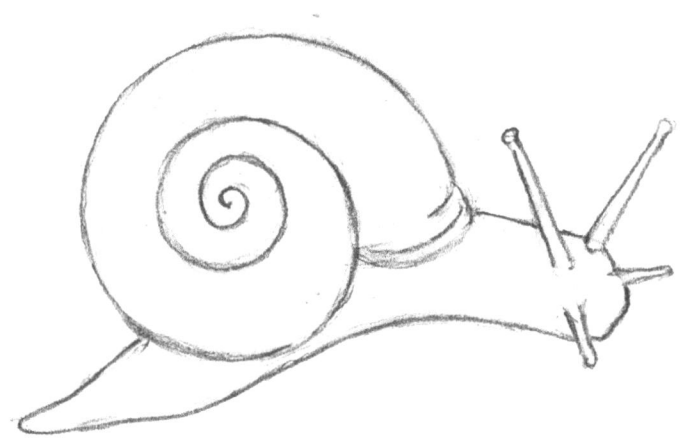

Use this sheet to transfer the image to your sheet of 140# hot press
watercolor paper.

Simple Snail Blending Exercise

Colors Used: Permanent White, Burnt Umber, Ultramarine Blue

This first exercise will be practicing blending. For me,
this is one of the most important techniques to learn
when painting with gouache. Good blending can give
the feeling of reality to your painting. Areas should flow
into one another without a hard edge. Sometimes I
think I spend more time blending with a damp brush
than I do actually applying the paint.

(1)

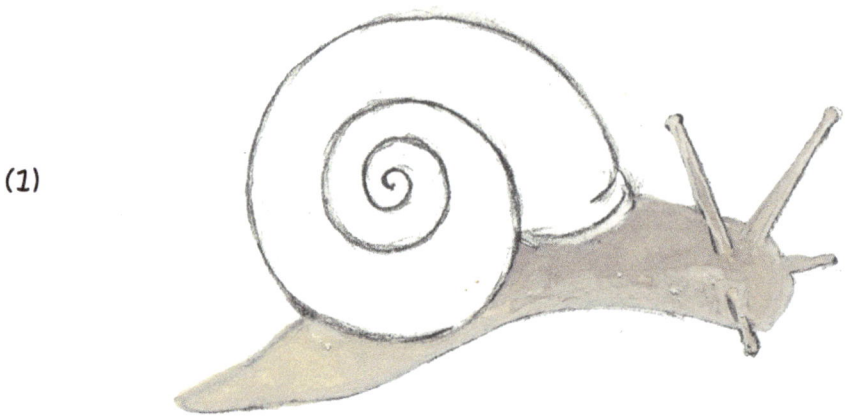

With a mixture of Permanent White tinted with Burnt Umber and
Ultramarine Blue to make a light gray, paint the body of the snail.

(2)

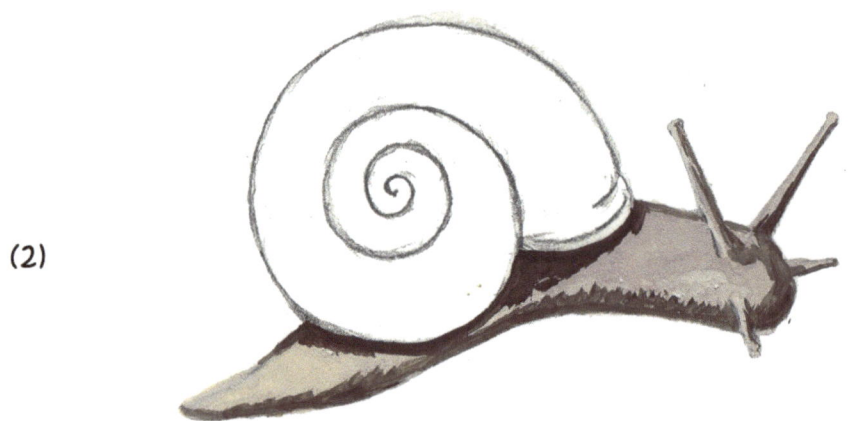

With a dark mixture of Burnt Umber and Ultramarine Blue, paint in the
shadow areas on the body.

Simple Snail Blending Exercise

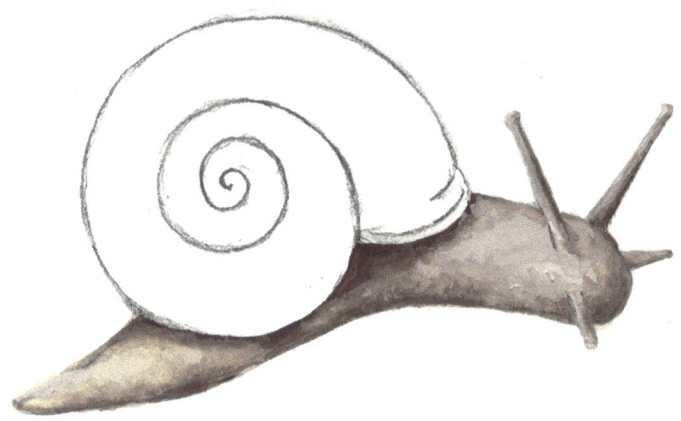

(3)

With a slightly damp brush, blend the dark areas into the light
areas, making a smooth transition.

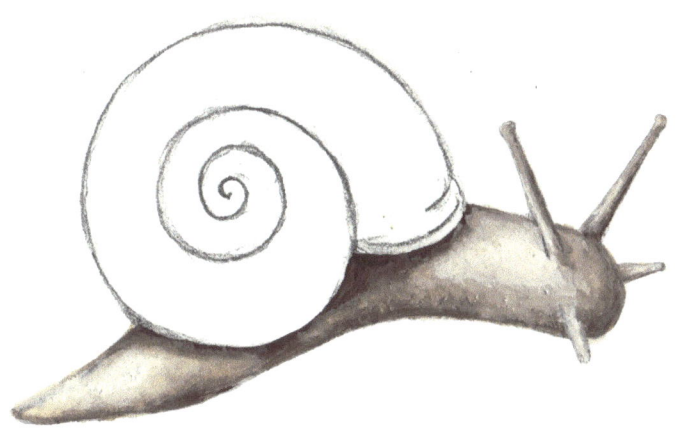

(4)

With pure Permanent White , paint highlights on each of the feelers,
the side of the head and the side of the tail. With a slightly damp
brush, gently blend the edges of the white into the gray to make
a smooth transition.

Simple Snail Blending Exercise

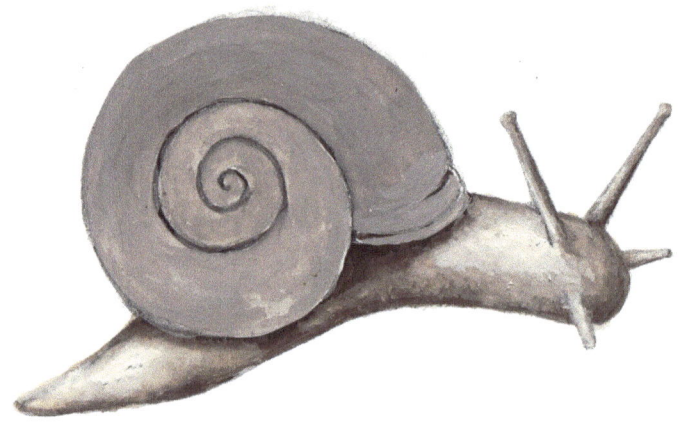

(5)

With a dark value mixture of Burnt Umber and Ultramarine Blue,
paint over the curvy interior lines of the shell so they're not lost
when you begin painting layers of gouache. Then, with a
medium value gray (Permanent White plus a little Burnt Umber
and Ultramarine Blue), paint the entire shell, being careful
not to paint over your guidelines.

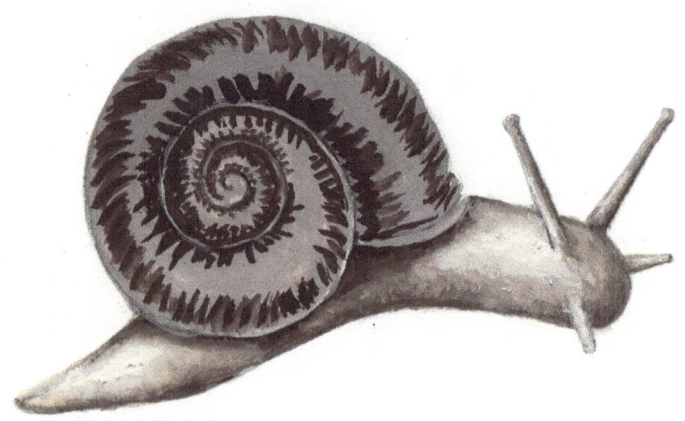

(6)

With a dark value of gray made by mixing Burnt Umber and
Ultramarine Blue, paint the shadows along the spiral of the shell.
Make your lines curve with the contours of the shell.

Simple Snail Blending Exercise

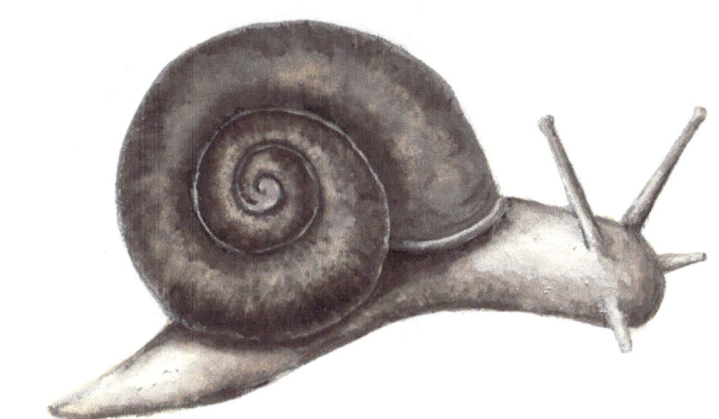

(7)

With a slightly damp brush, gently blend the darks into the light
areas to make a smooth transition. Stroke your brush in the
direction of the contours of the shell. Paint a white line
on the front edge of the shell, above the snail's neck. Blend it in.

HAVE FUN WITH THIS PROJECT!

It's not necessary to use the colors I've demonstrated here.
If you'd like, use red or blue or green, anything you want.
Just be sure that you use a varied value range so
that you can show contrast in the form of the snail.
Be creative! Add racing stripes, eyelashes, a smiley face.
The main focus of this lesson is to learn to blend
the gouache and make subtle transitions.

American Toad

Colors Used: Permanent White, Burnt Umber, Ultramarine Blue, Olive Green, Brilliant Yellow, Burnt Sienna

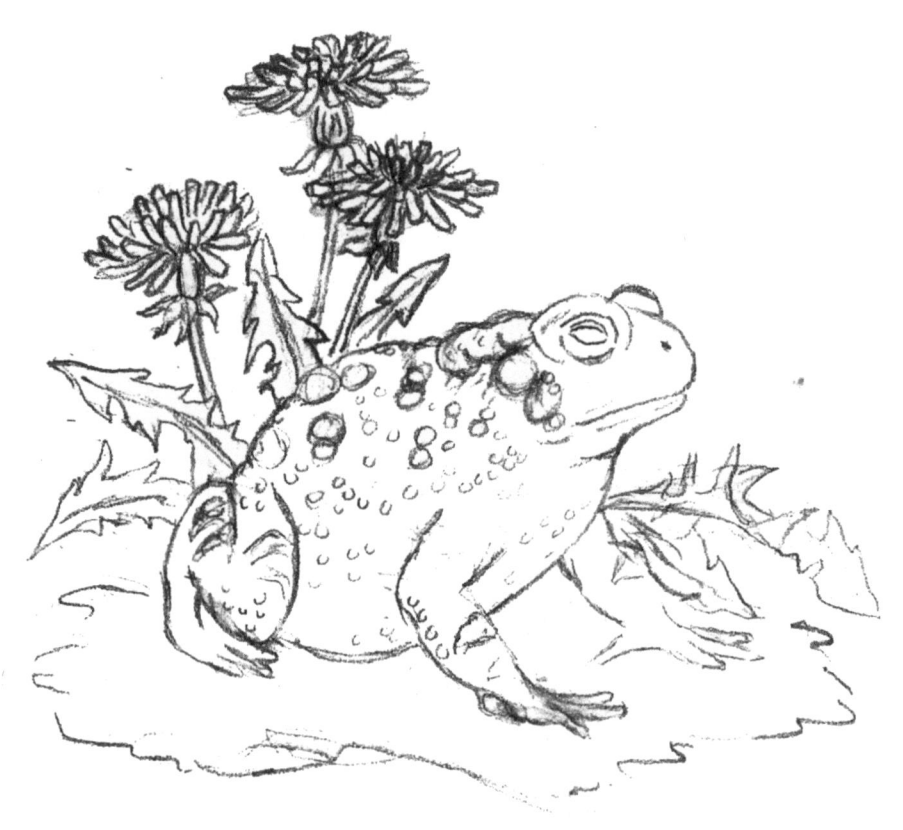

Use this sheet to transfer the image to your sheet of 140# hot press watercolor paper.

American Toad

Colors Used: Permanent White, Burnt Umber, Ultramarine Blue, Olive Green
Brilliant Yellow, Burnt Sienna

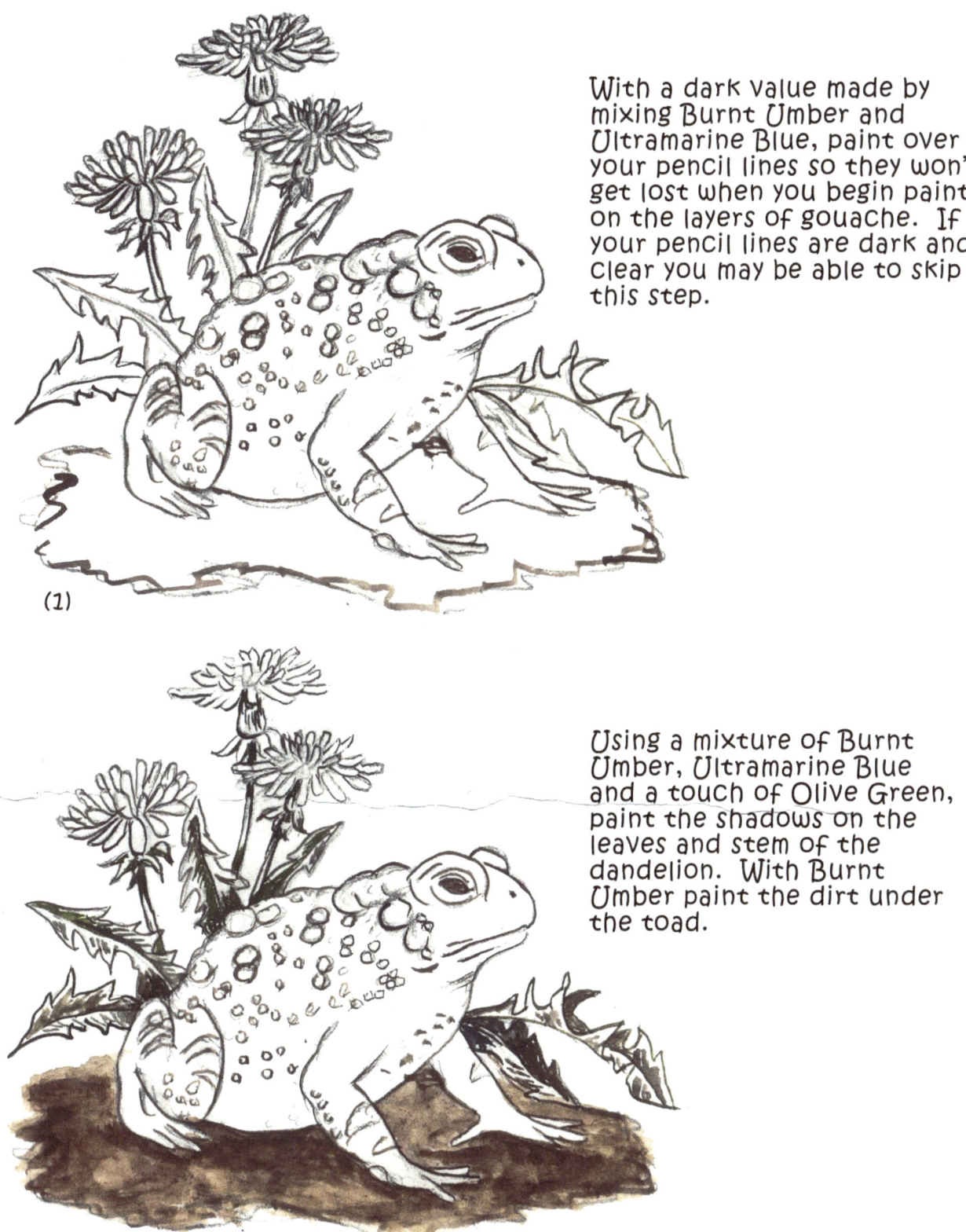

With a dark value made by mixing Burnt Umber and Ultramarine Blue, paint over your pencil lines so they won't get lost when you begin painting on the layers of gouache. If your pencil lines are dark and clear you may be able to skip this step.

(1)

Using a mixture of Burnt Umber, Ultramarine Blue and a touch of Olive Green, paint the shadows on the leaves and stem of the dandelion. With Burnt Umber paint the dirt under the toad.

American Toad

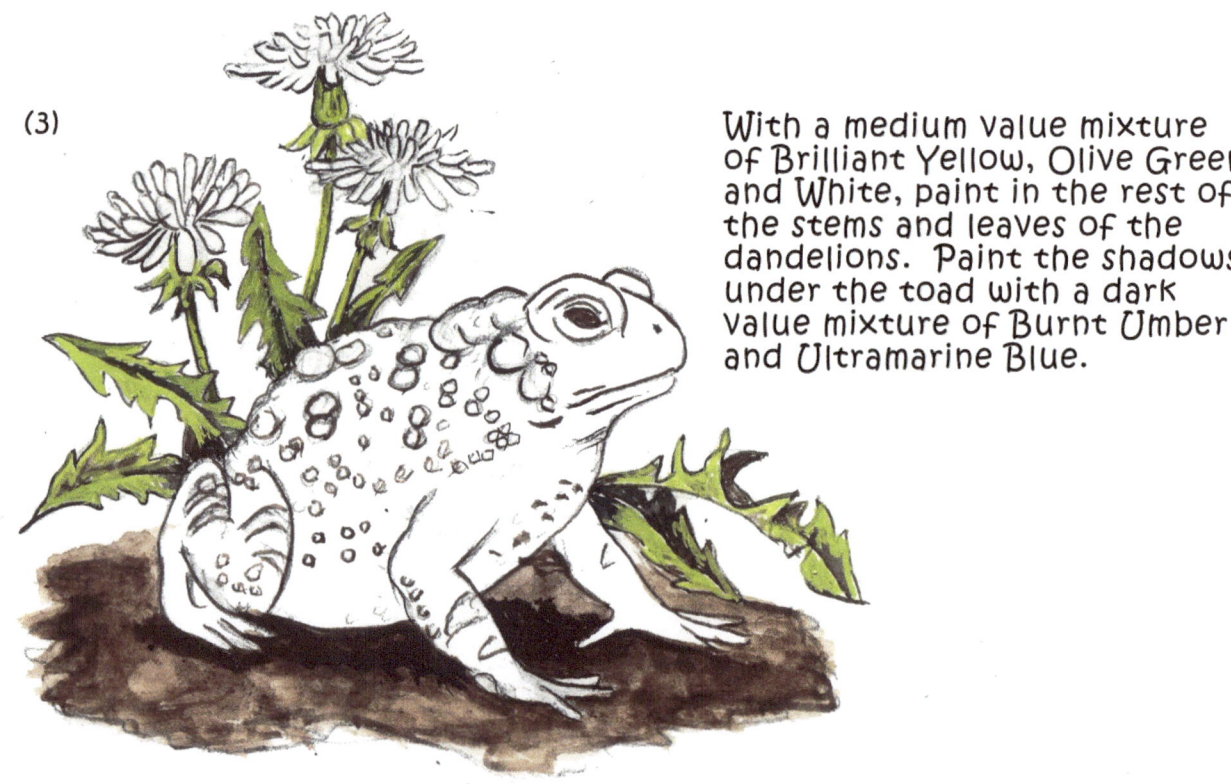

(3)

With a medium value mixture of Brilliant Yellow, Olive Green and White, paint in the rest of the stems and leaves of the dandelions. Paint the shadows under the toad with a dark value mixture of Burnt Umber and Ultramarine Blue.

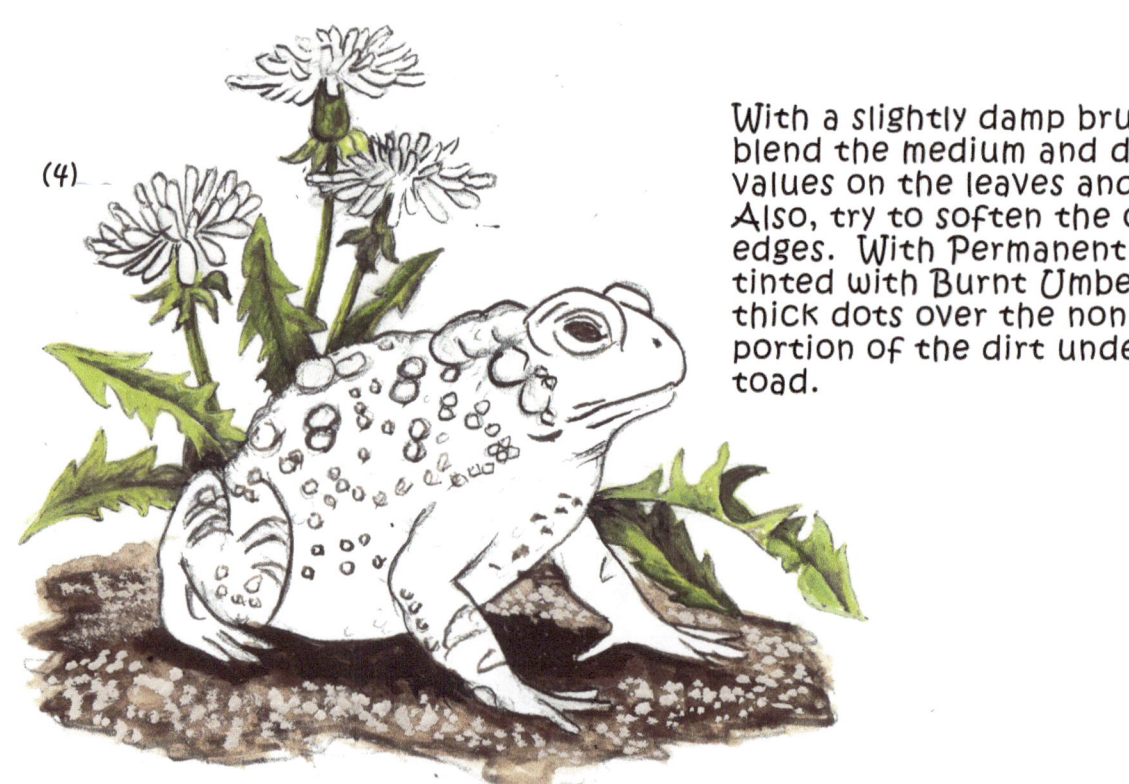

(4)

With a slightly damp brush, blend the medium and dark values on the leaves and stems. Also, try to soften the outside edges. With Permanent White tinted with Burnt Umber, paint thick dots over the non shadow portion of the dirt under the toad.

American Toad

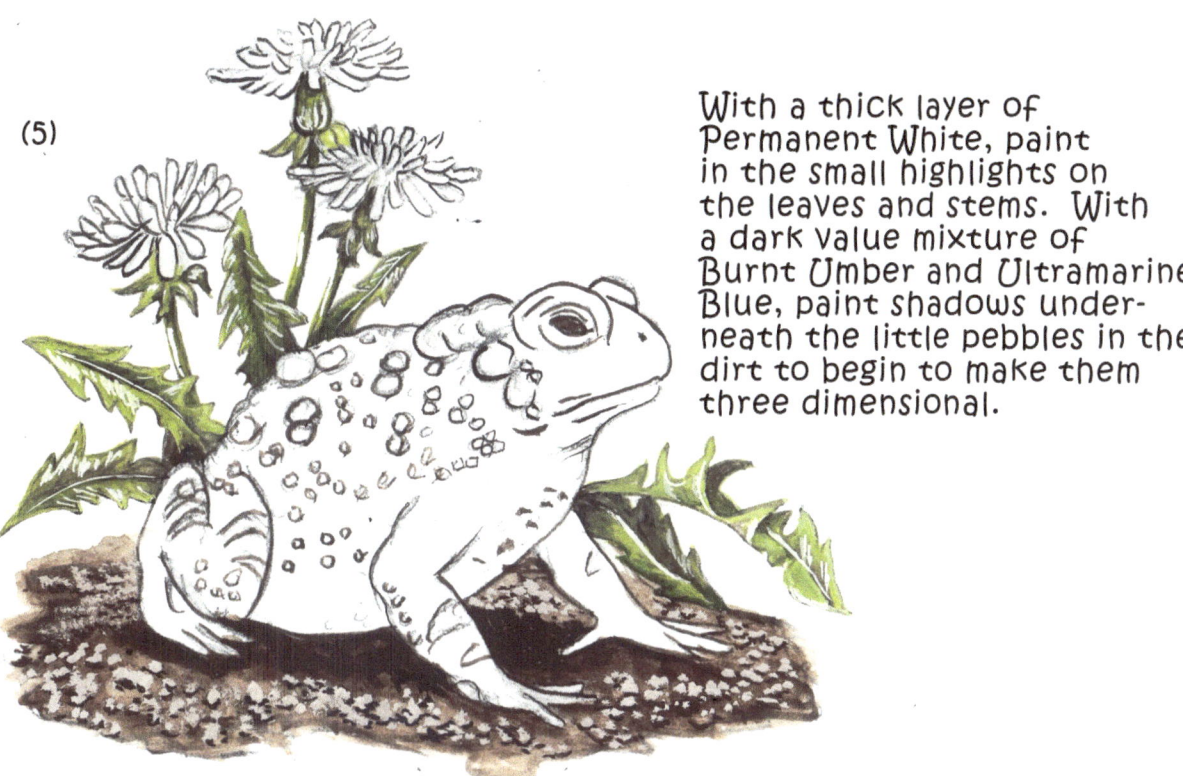

(5)

With a thick layer of Permanent White, paint in the small highlights on the leaves and stems. With a dark value mixture of Burnt Umber and Ultramarine Blue, paint shadows underneath the little pebbles in the dirt to begin to make them three dimensional.

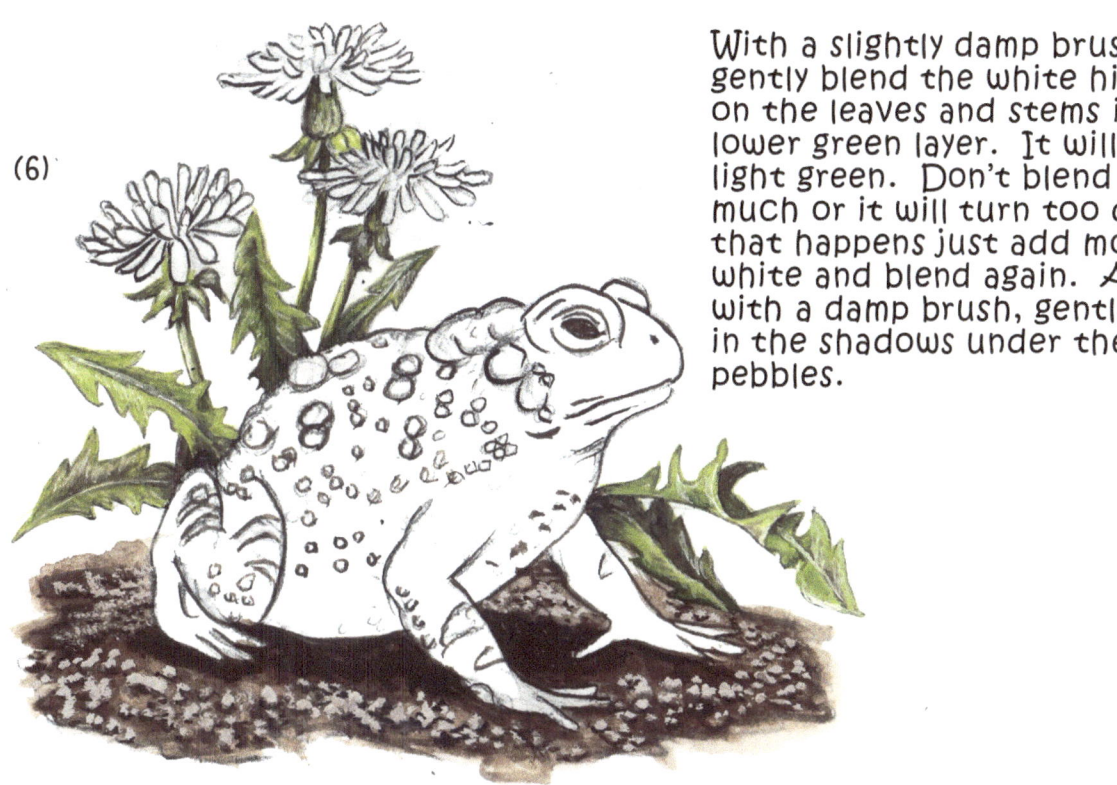

(6)

With a slightly damp brush, gently blend the white highlights on the leaves and stems into the lower green layer. It will turn light green. Don't blend it too much or it will turn too dark. If that happens just add more white and blend again. Also, with a damp brush, gently blend in the shadows under the tiny pebbles.

American Toad

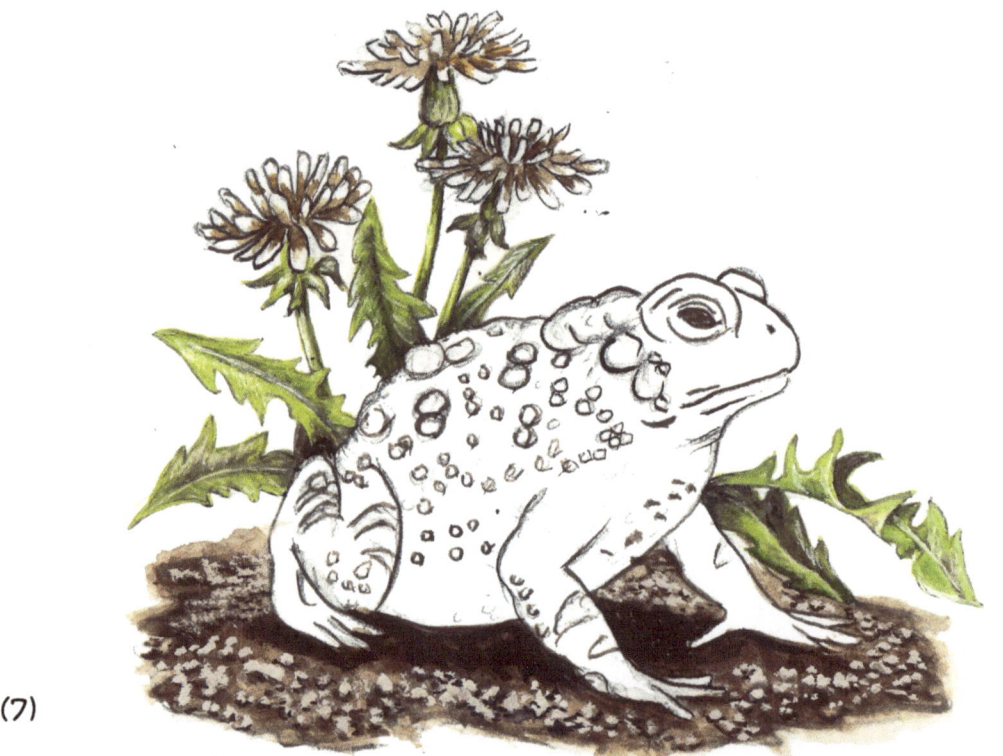

(7)

Dandelion heads -- With a dark value of Burnt Umber and Burnt Sienna, paint the shadows on the petals.

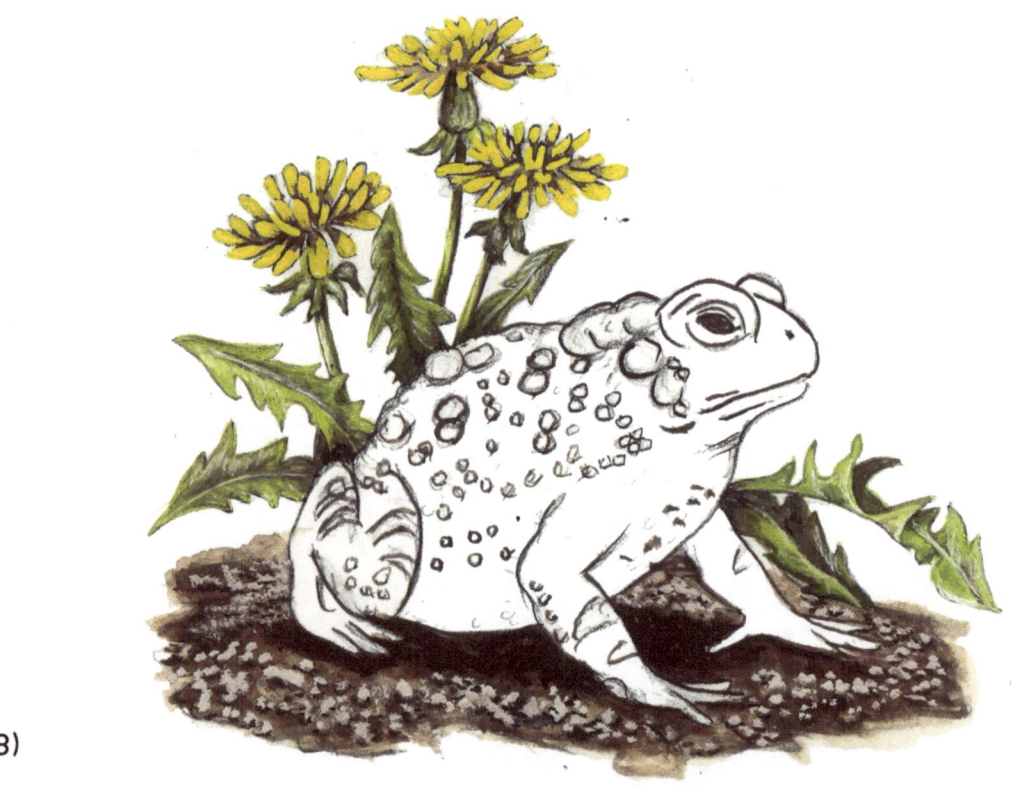

(8)

Paint the remaining portions of the petals with a thick layer of Brilliant Yellow.

American Toad

(9)

With a slightly damp brush, blend the yellow into the shadow color. Make a smooth transition. You may have to add more yellow and blend again if it gets too dark. Try to paint the yellow right up to the edges of the petals so only a hair's breadth of the dark outline shows. When you're finished, touch the tips of the front petals with White to highlight them. Blend gently.

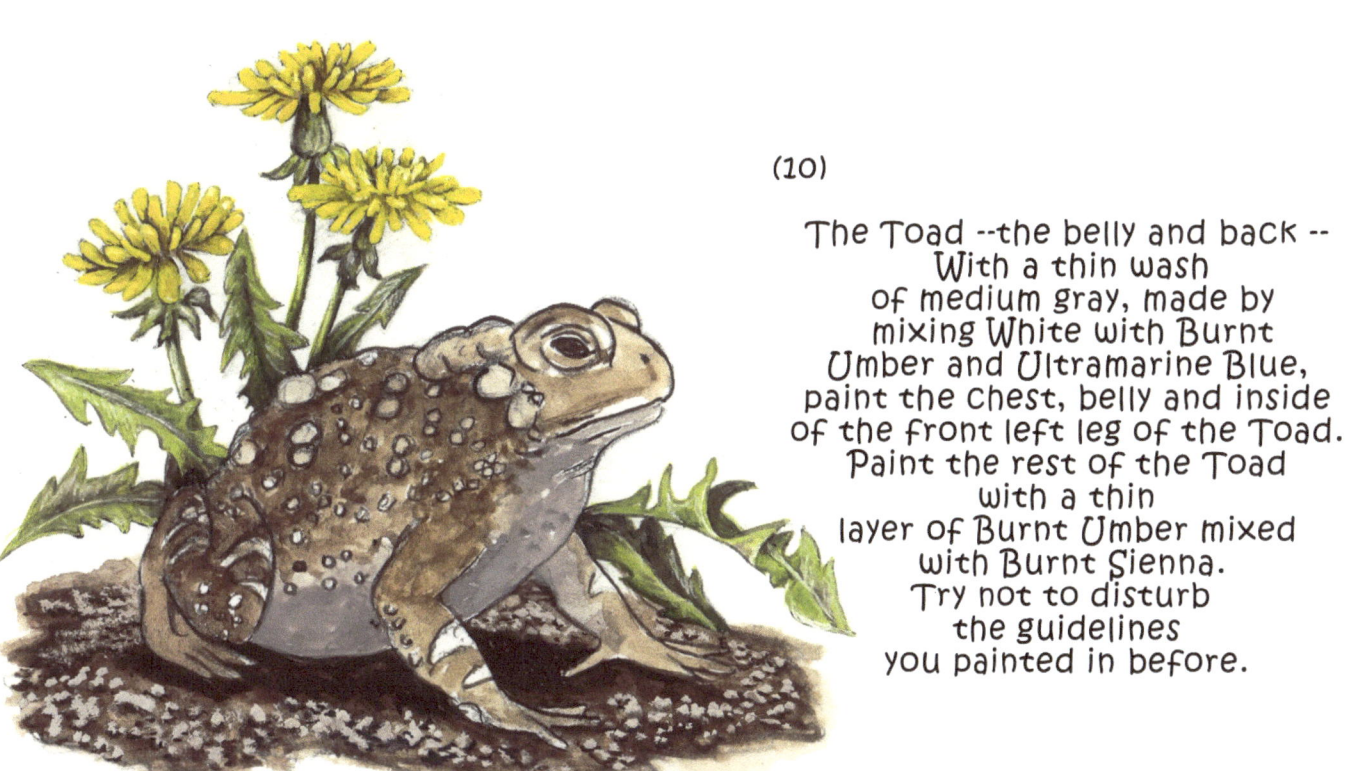

(10)

The Toad --the belly and back -- With a thin wash of medium gray, made by mixing White with Burnt Umber and Ultramarine Blue, paint the chest, belly and inside of the front left leg of the Toad. Paint the rest of the Toad with a thin layer of Burnt Umber mixed with Burnt Sienna. Try not to disturb the guidelines you painted in before.

American Toad

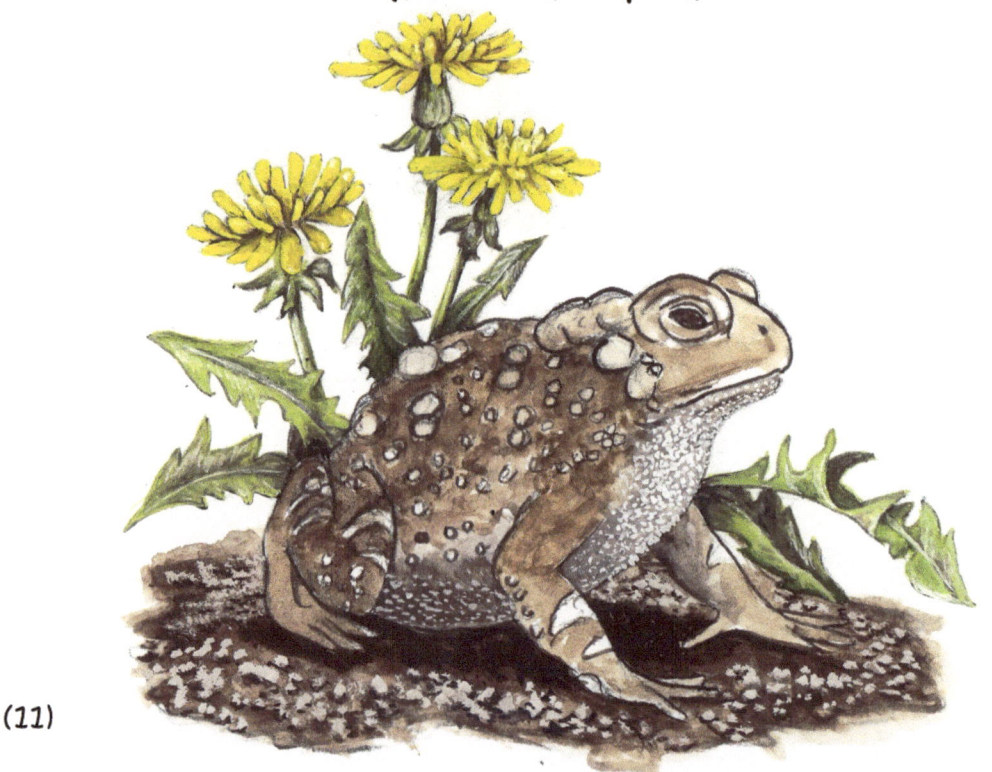

(11)

Darken the shadow on the underside of the belly in front of the back leg and at the top of the left front leg. With the tip of your brush, texture the underside of the Toad with small dots of paint, pure white under the chin and on the chest and light gray in the shadow areas.

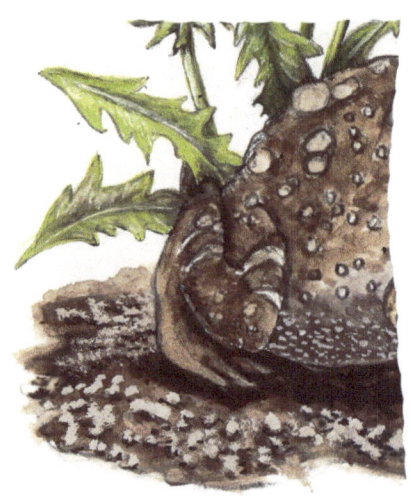

(12)

Back Leg -- With a dark vlue of brown made by mixing Burnt Umber and Ultramarine Blue, darken the shadow on the body in front of the leg and also underneath the lower portion of the rear leg.

American Toad

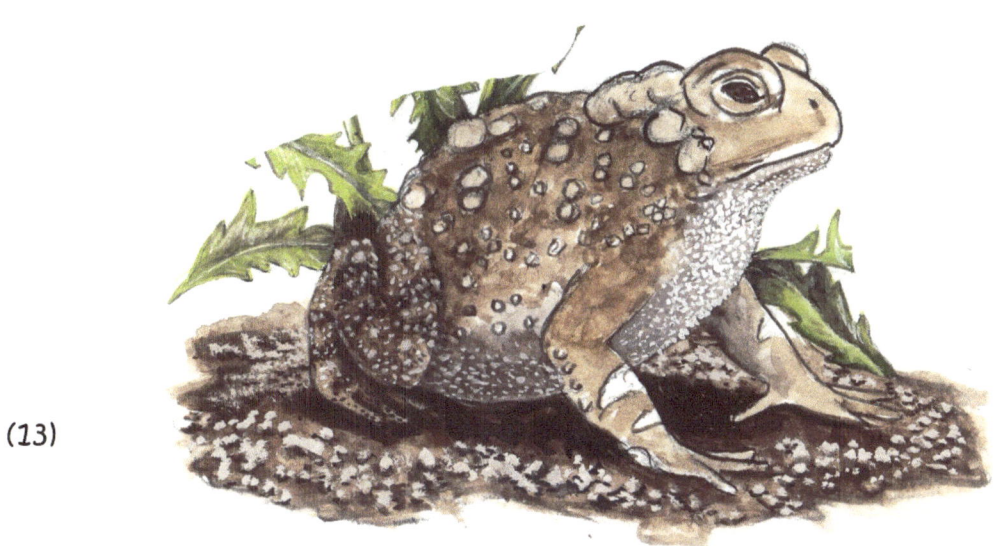

(13)

Chest, Belly and Back Leg -- With Burnt Umber, paint in the dark areas on the back leg. Make sure the edges are softened. Using thick, Permanent White tinted with Burnt Umber, take the tip of your brush and paint small dots. Don't make the dots all the same size or in too regular of a pattern. Soften their edges so they don't look pasted on. Put a few very tiny Burnt Umber specks on the long toes.

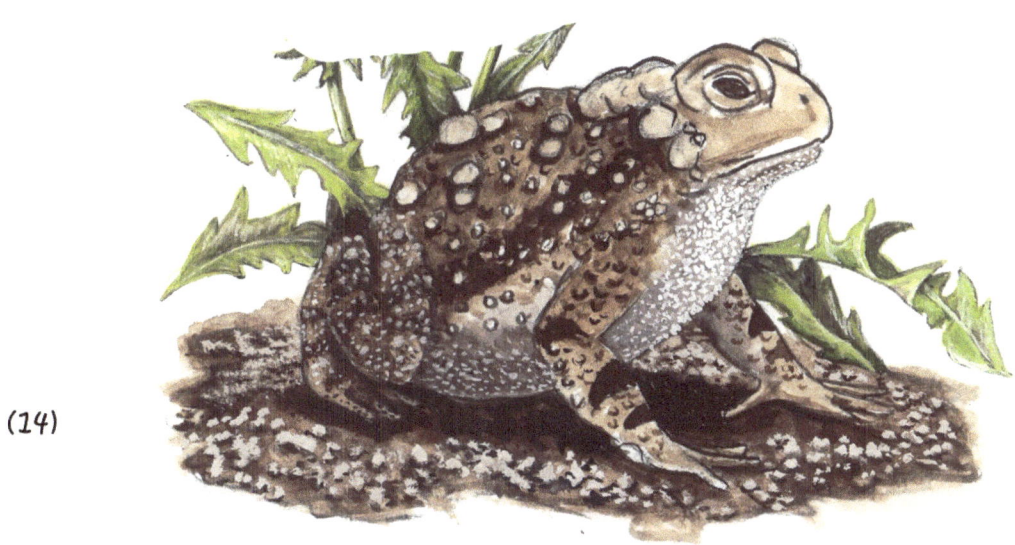

(14)

With Burnt Umber, paint the dark areas down the side of the Toad along with the dark stripes on the front legs. Also, paint dark shadows on the lower side of the bumps and "warts." Paint them as small seimicircles.

American Toad

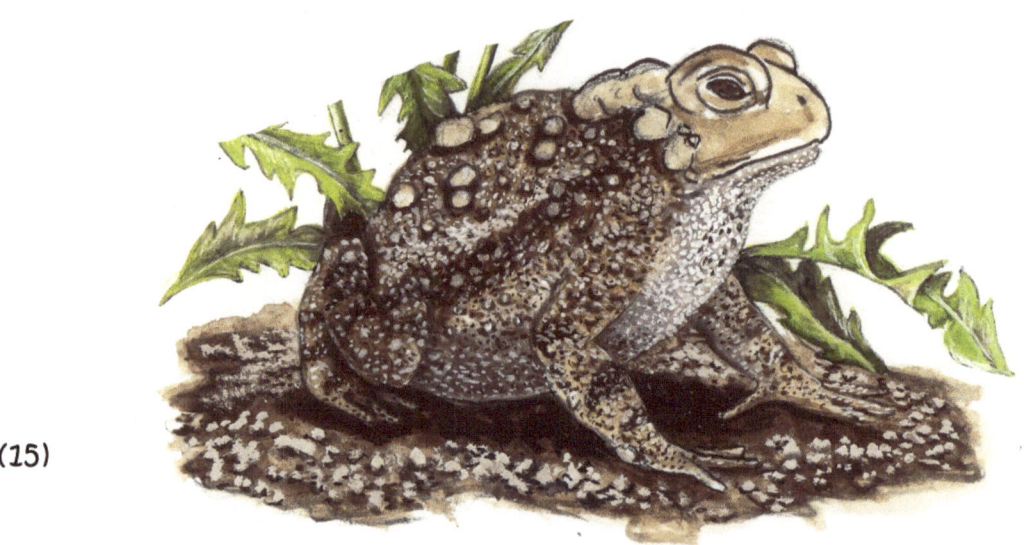

(15)

With Permanent White tinted with Burnt Umber, stipple in the tiny dots on the body and front legs of the Toad. Blend their edges a little so they don't look too hard edged and pasted on. With Burnt Umber, make tiny dark stipples over the body and front legs. Paint dark spots on the chest of the Toad.

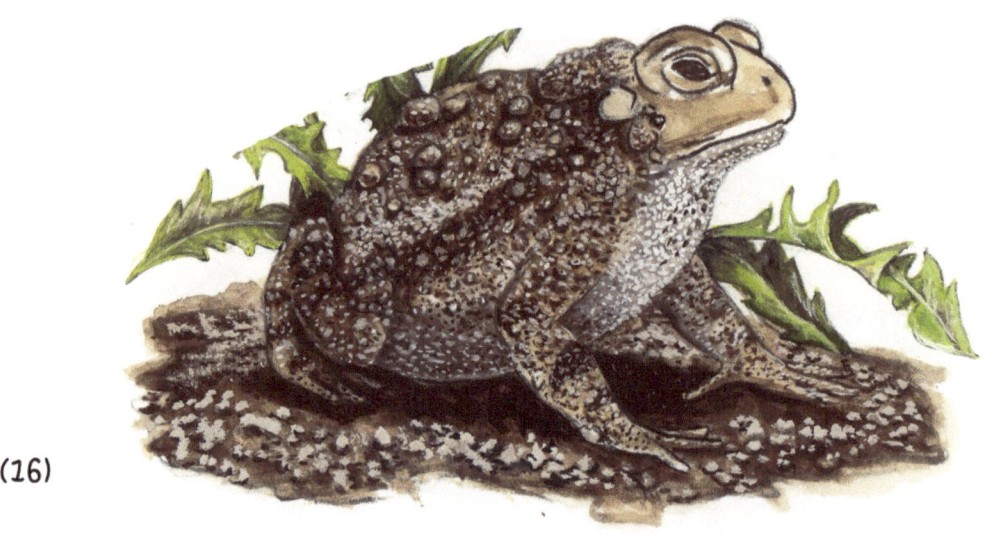

(16)

For the large bumps and glands on the Toad's back and neck, use Burnt Umber to shade the left and lower sides. Make darker Burnt Umber dots to detail the bumps and mix White with a little Burnt Umber to make the lighter dots for highlights. The circle behind the Toad's eye is the ear drum, the tympanium, not a bump.

American Toad

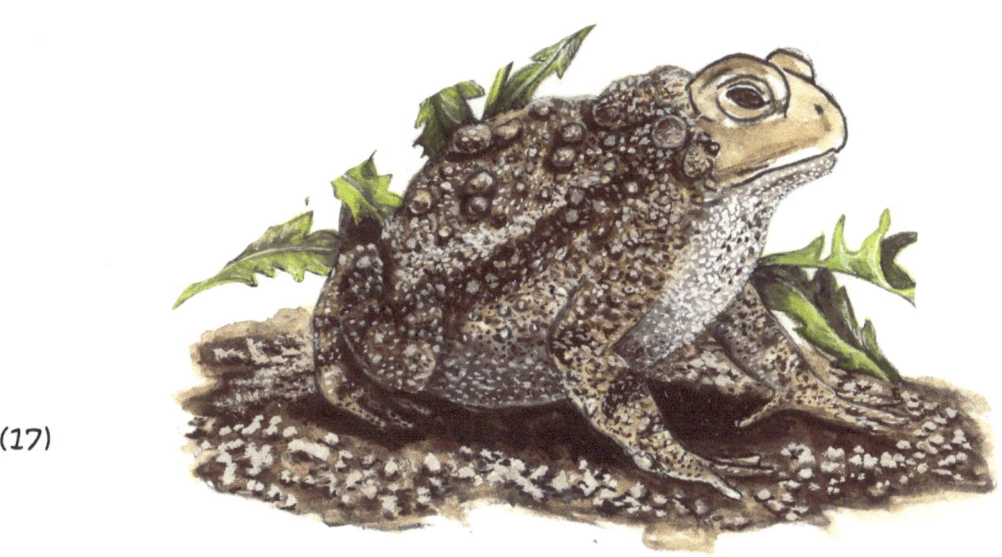

(17)

Ear Drum (Tympanium) - With a light gray (White tinted with a little Burnt Umber and Ultramarine Blue), paint the round ear drum. Make a line around it with Burnt Umber and blend the edges slightly to take the hard edge off. With Burnt Umber, shade in the top part of the ear drum, making a smooth transition.

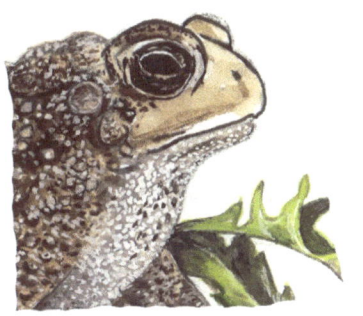

(18)

Eye -- With a dark mixture of Burnt Umber and Ultramarine Blue, paint in the pupil of the eye. With Burnt Umber paint in the rest of the dark areas around the eye.

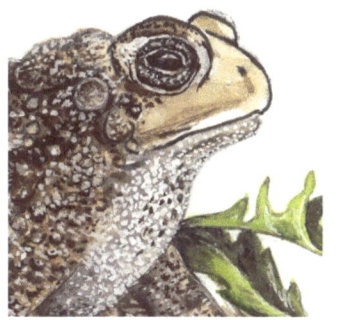

(19)

With Permanent White, paint the circle around the pupil. With White tinted with a little Burnt Umber paint tiny dots in the dark area around the pupil. With White, paint a highlight on the eye and gently blend the edges with a damp brush.

American Toad

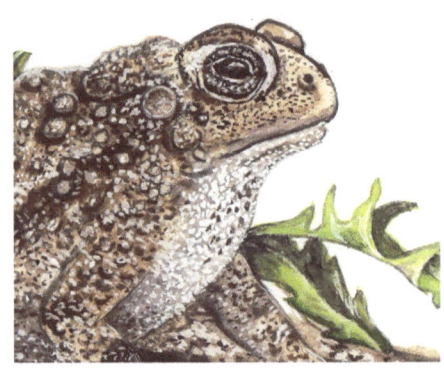

(20)

Head -- Paint the edge of te upper lip medium gray and blend it into the dark line below to take the hard edge off. Darken the nostril with the darkest value of Burnt Umber and Ultramaine Blue. Make a Burnt Umber semicircle around the nostril and blend it in. With Burnt Umber, paint tiny dots on the head.

(21)

With Permanent White, paint small dots on the head to create a texture. Make more along the upper lip to make it appear lighter. With a slightly damp brush, blend them in a tiny bit. Soften the outside edges of the whole Toad so it doesn't look pasted on the paper.

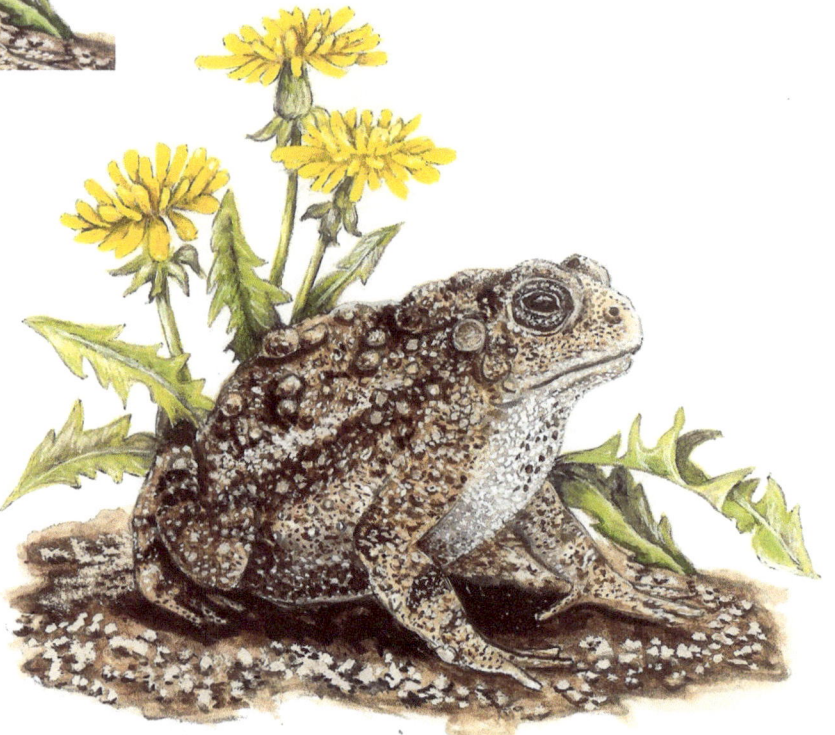

(22)

Now stand back and take a look at your painting. Make any needed value adjustments. On this American Toad I went back and redefined some dark areas to get a little more range of value.
. . . And you're done!!

Eastern Box Turtle

Colors Used: Permanent White,
Burnt Umber, Burnt Sienna, Primary Red,
Olive Green, Ultramarine Blue, Brilliant Yellow

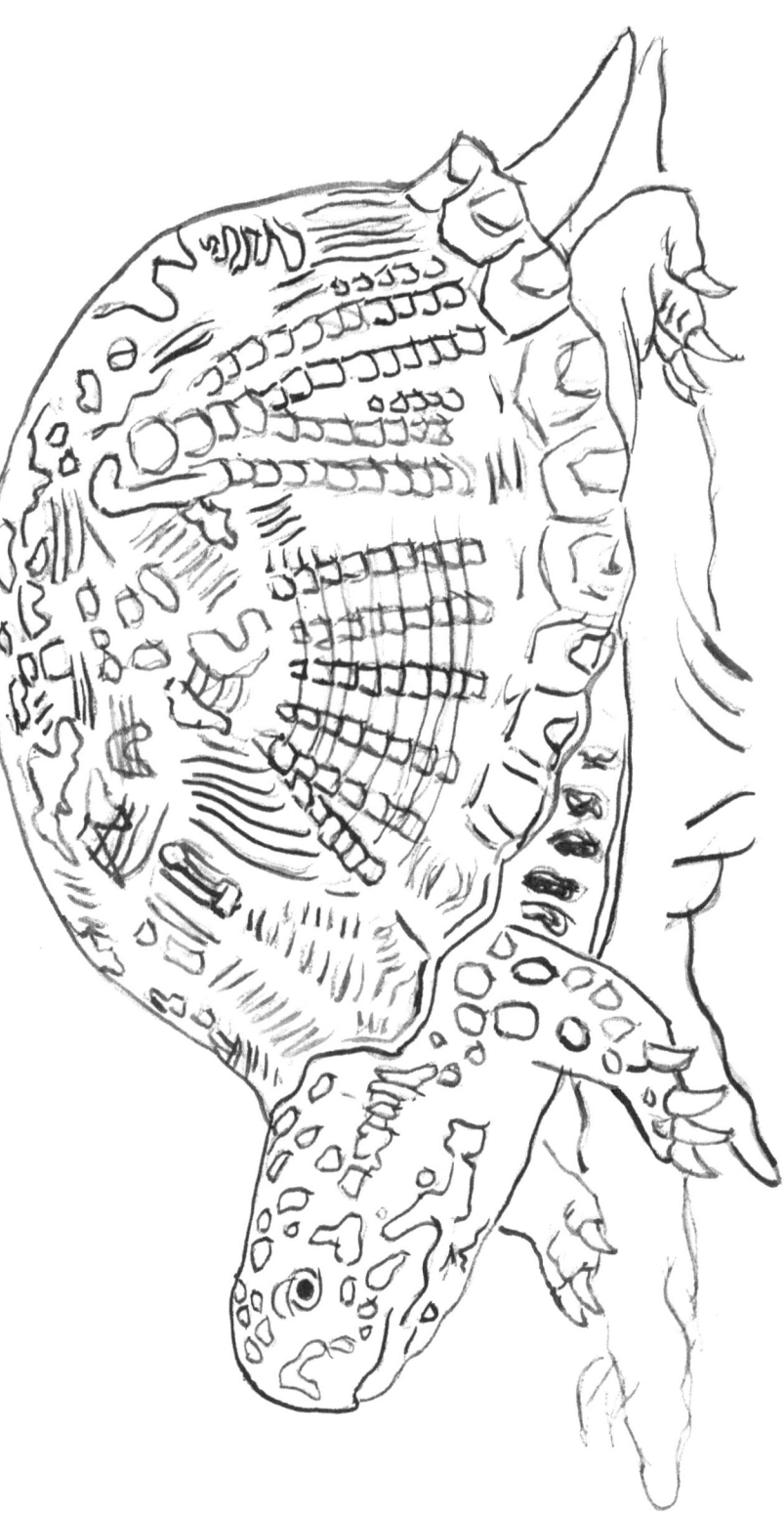

Use this sheet to transfer the image to your sheet of 140# hot press watercolor paper.

Eastern Box Turtle

Colors Used: Permanent White,
Burnt Umber, Burnt Sienna, Primary Red,
Olive Green, Ultramarine Blue, Brilliant Yellow

(1)   Go over your pencil lines with a dark mixture of
Burnt Umber added to Ultramarine Blue so
that they don't disappear completely when you
begin adding layers of gouache.

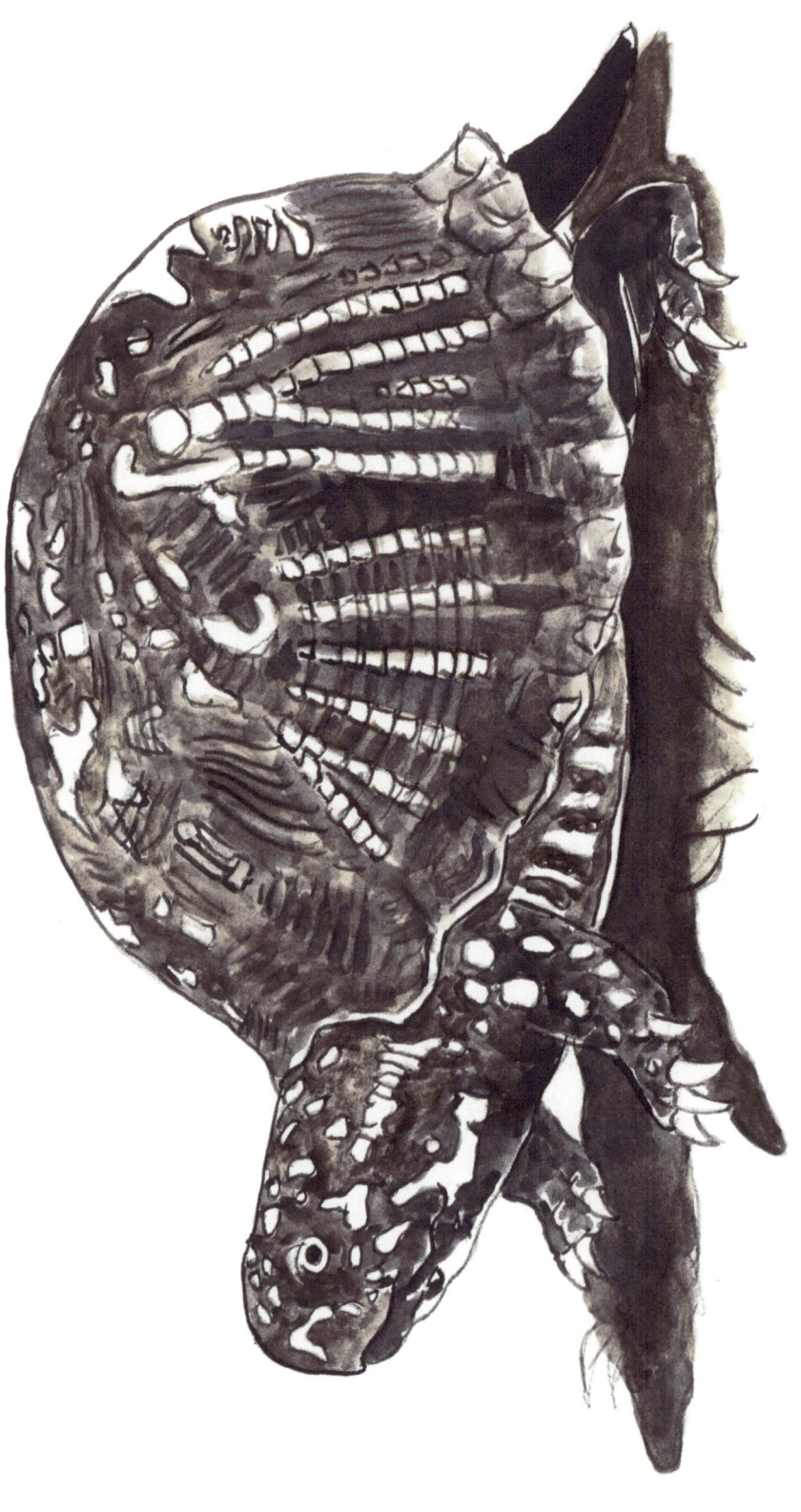

(2)

Shadows -- With a thin wash of a mixture of Burnt Umber and Ultramarine Blue, paint in the shadow
under the turtle. Don't worry about putting the grass in yet. That will be added at the end.
With the same thin, dark wash, paint in the dark areas of the turtle, being careful not to lose
your lines.

Eastern Box Turtle   The Eye

For demonstration purposes I'll be breaking the turtle down into sections to show the detailing.

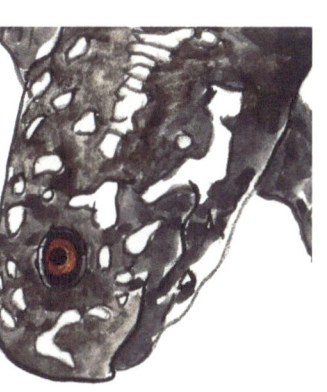

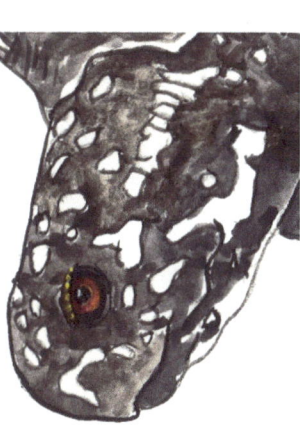

(4) With Brilliant Yellow, paint a very thin rim around the lower part of the pupil. Also, use Yellow to highlight the lower left side of the iris. Using a slightly damp brush, blend the yellow into the red to soften the edges. Also, soften the edge where the red meets the black area outside of the iris.

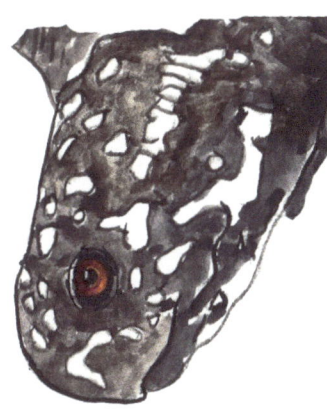

(6)   With a dark value of Burnt Umber and Ultramarine Blue, make a dark line over the top of the eye, touching the top of the red iris. With Brilliant Yellow, paint tiny dots on top of the black line. Gently blend the dots a little with a damp brush to soften the edges.

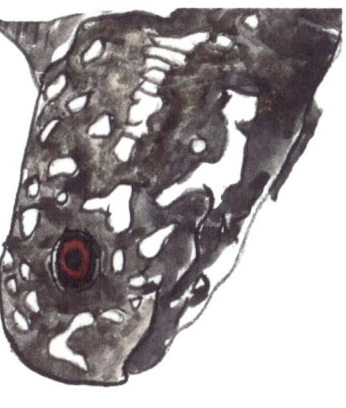

(3) The Eye -- Darken the pupil of the eye with a thick coat of the Burnt Umber and Ultramarine Blue mixture. Make the pupil as round as possible. With Primary Red paint the iris of the eye. Also, darken the area around the iris with the Burnt Umber and Ultramarine Blue mixture.

(5) With Burnt Umber, shadow the top part of the red iris. With White tinted with Ultramarine Blue, paint in tiny highlights in the pupil. Make sure the areas are blended with a damp brush so there are no hard edges.

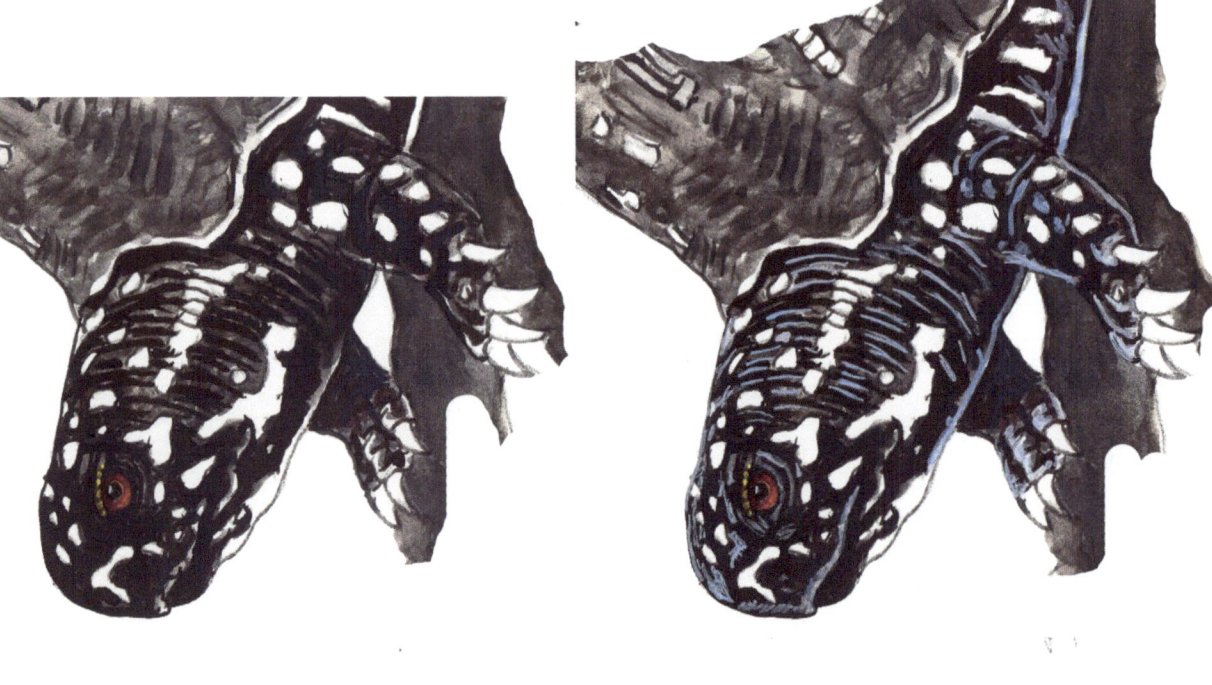

(7)   Using a thick, dark mixture of Burnt Umber and Ultramarine Blue, darken the darkest areas on the turtle's head and front legs. Make your brush strokes follow the contours of the form. Don't completely cover the first thin layer. Don't paint over the tops of the wrinkes where you will eventually be painting the highlights.

(8)   At this point still ignore all the yellow spots on the turtle. Tint thick, creamy White gouache with a little Ultramarine Blue. Paint in the places where the light hits the upper portions of the wrinkles on the neck, the head both legs and make a line on the lower portion of the shell (the plastron) so that it will show up.

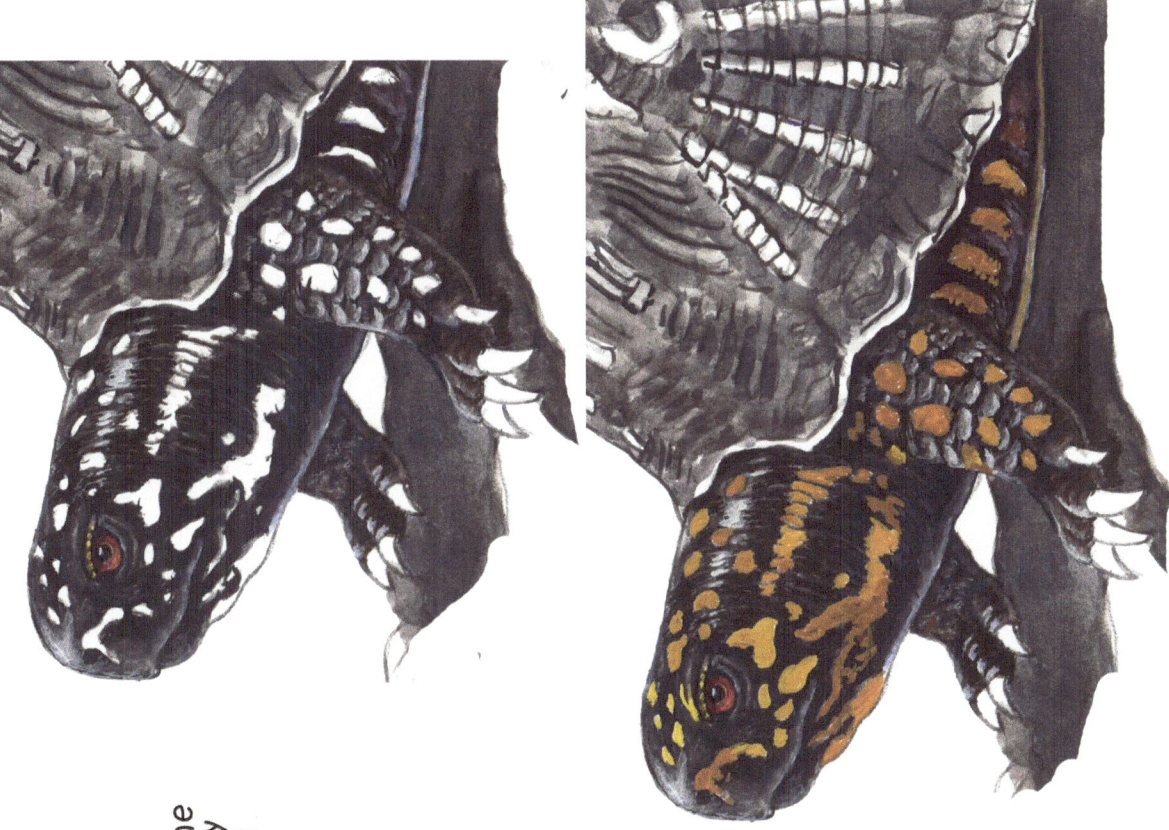

(9)

With a slightly damp brush, blend the edges of the highlights into the dark areas. You will probably have to add the tinted white mixture again and reblend in the places where the lights get too dark after blending. This is a back and forth process. Take your time. Soften all the outside edges so the turtle doesn't look pasted on the paper.

(10)

With a thick mixture of Brilliany Yellow with a little Burnt Sienna added, paint in the yellow spots.

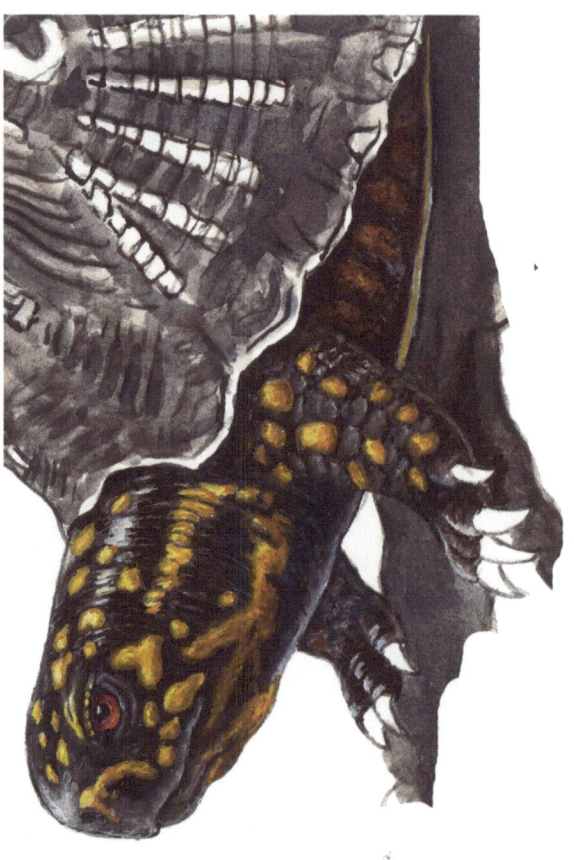

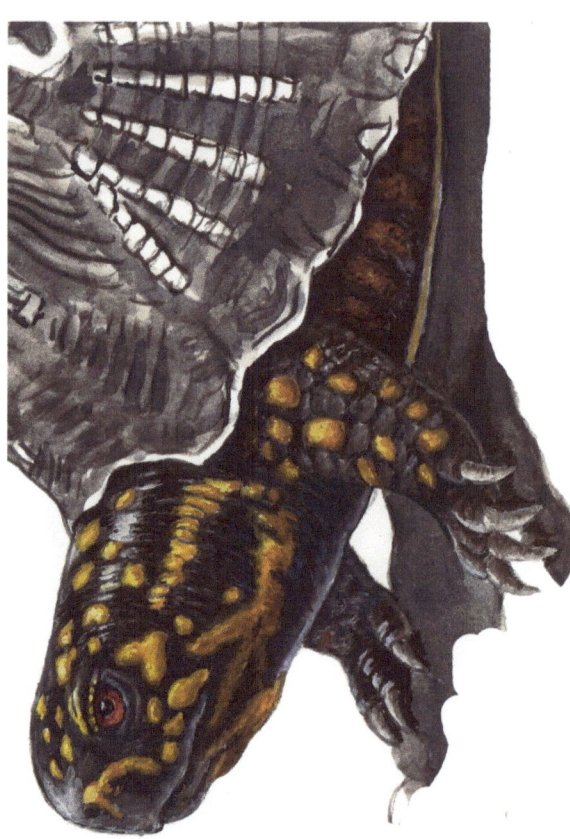

(11) Shade the yellow spots by highlighting the upper ones with Brilliant Yellow mixed with White, and add a bit of Burnt Umber plus Brilliant Yellow to darken the lower ones. Gently blend all the edges of the spots so they don't look pasted on.

(12) Toe nails -- Paint the toe nails a medium value gray with a mixture of Permanent White and a little bit of Burnt Umber and Ultramarine Blue. With a dark value of the Burnt Umber and Ultramarine Blue mixture, paint the shadows of the nails. With Permanent White paint the highlights on top. Then, with a slightly damp brush, gently blend the areas together. IF you lose the top highlights just add more White and gently blend again.

Eastern Box Turtle

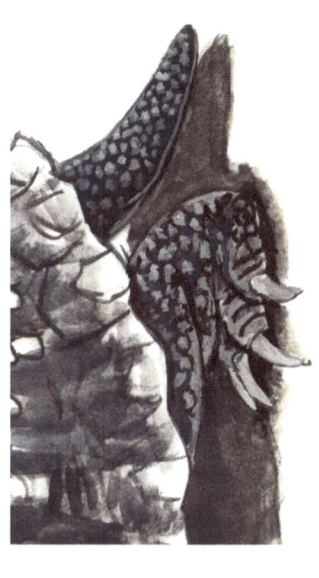

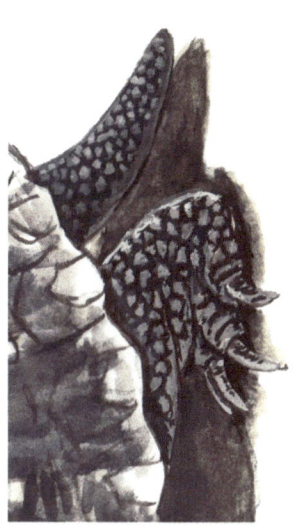

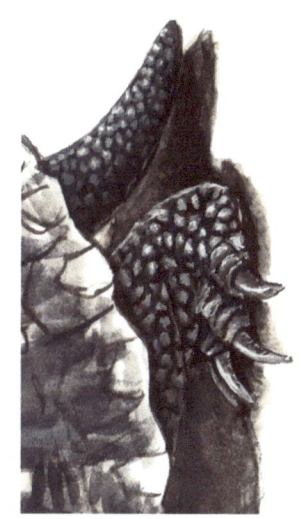

(13) With a medium value of gray made by mixing Burnt Umber, Ultramarine Blue and Permanent White, paint an irregular pattern of dots on the tail and back leg. Also paint the toe nails.

(14) With the darkest value of your Burnt Umber and Ultramarine Blue mixture, paint around each gray segment. Also paint shadows on the toe nails.

(15) With pure Permanent White, paint tiny highlights on the light gray dots. Then with a slightly damp brush, gently blend to soften the hard edges. Blend more on the lower areas away from the light to form shadows. You may have to add more White and rebland if the highlights get blended out.

Eastern Box Turtle

The Shell

(16) Shell -- With the darkest value of *Burnt Umber* and *Ultramarine Blue*, paint the dark lines in the pattern on the turtle's shell. Observe carefully. Ignore the yellow spots and leave them white.

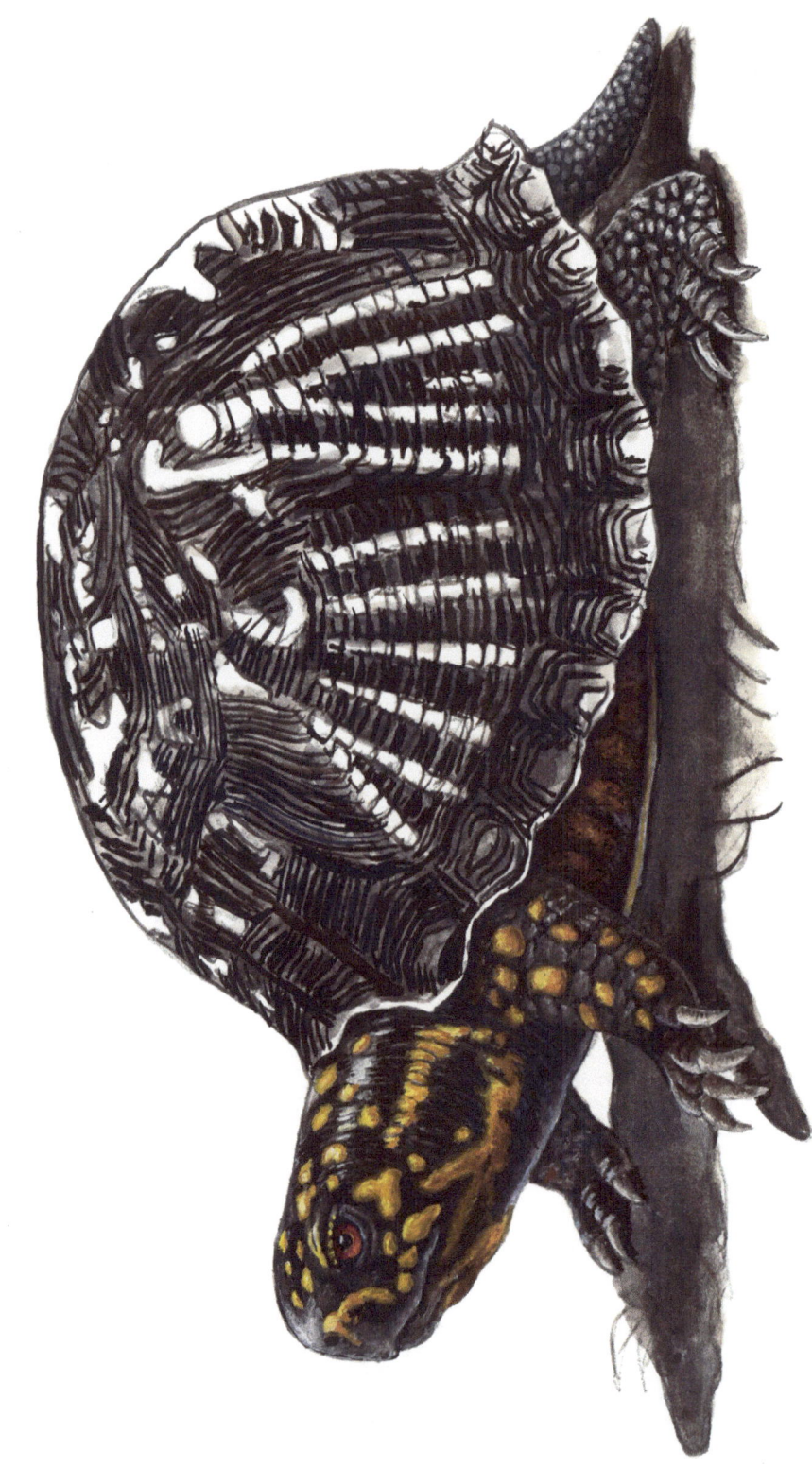

Eastern Box Turtle

The Shell

(17)   With Permanent White tinted with the Burnt Umber and Ultramarine Blue mixture to make a light gray, paint in the top rims of the ridges of the shell.

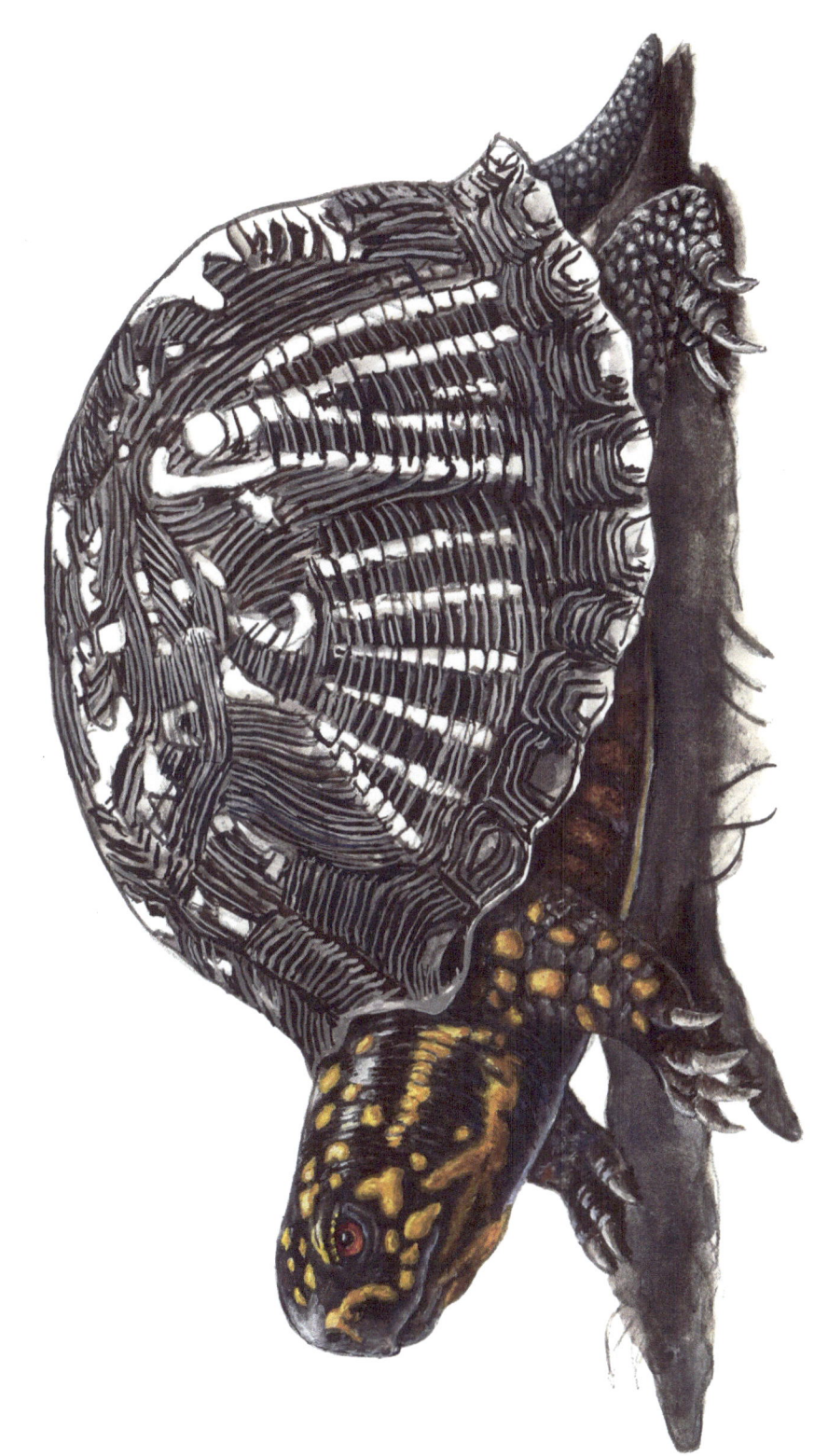

Eastern Box Turtle

The Shell

(18)   With a slightly damp brush, begin blending the lightest areas into the darks, making a smooth transition. You will probably have to keep adding more of the dark and light values as you go along and reblend until you get a smooth transition between them and still retain a good contrast. This will be time consuming.

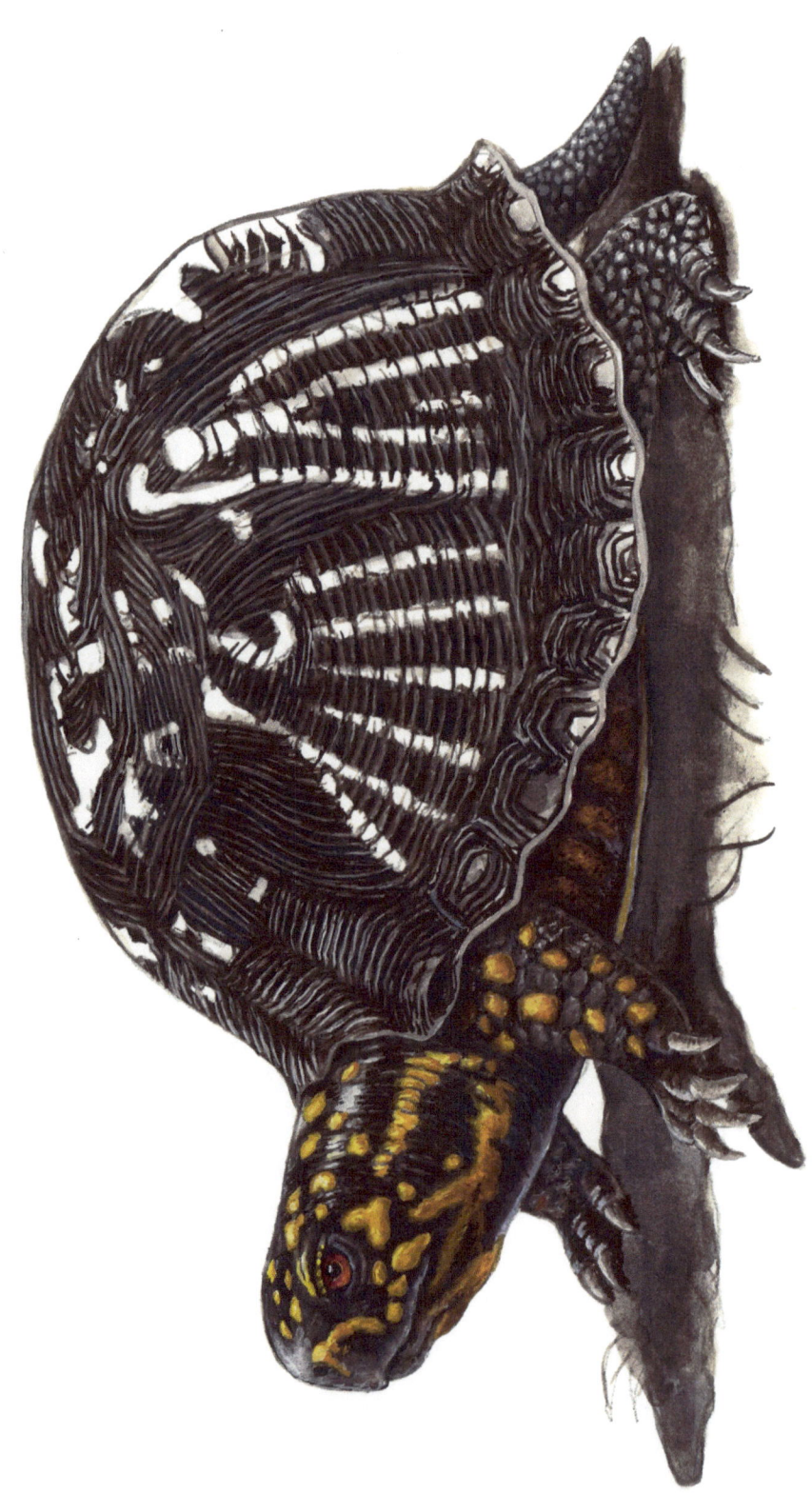

Eastern Box Turtle

The Shell

(19) Paint the yellow spots with a mixture of Brilliant Yellow and Burnt Sienna.

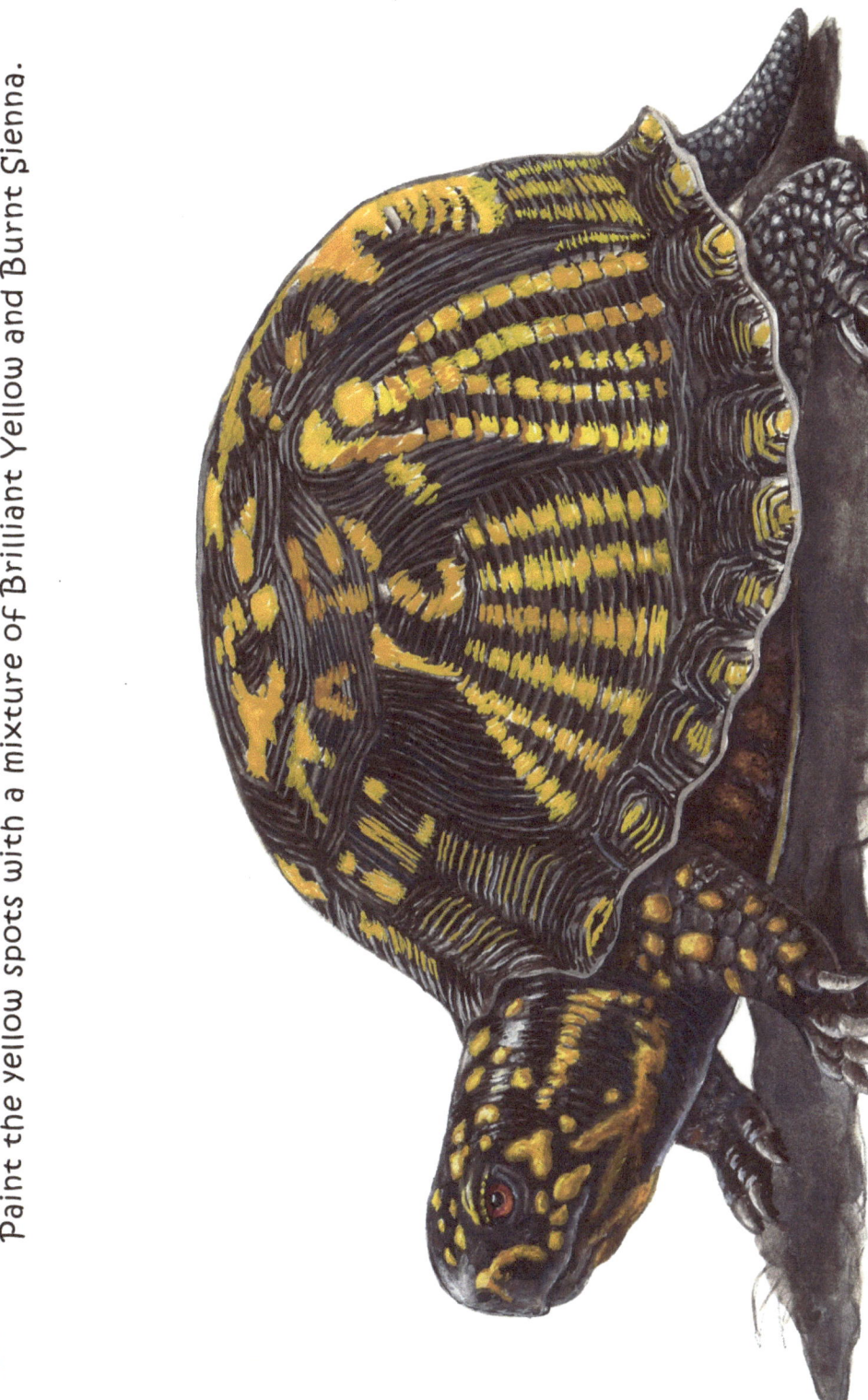

Eastern Box Turtle

The Shell

(20)   Using Permanent White tinted with Brilliant Yellow, highlight the yellow spots on the top of the shell and on top of the ridges. With Brilliant Yellow shaded with Burnt Sienna and a little Burnt Umber, shade the lower part of the yellow spots and the ridges.

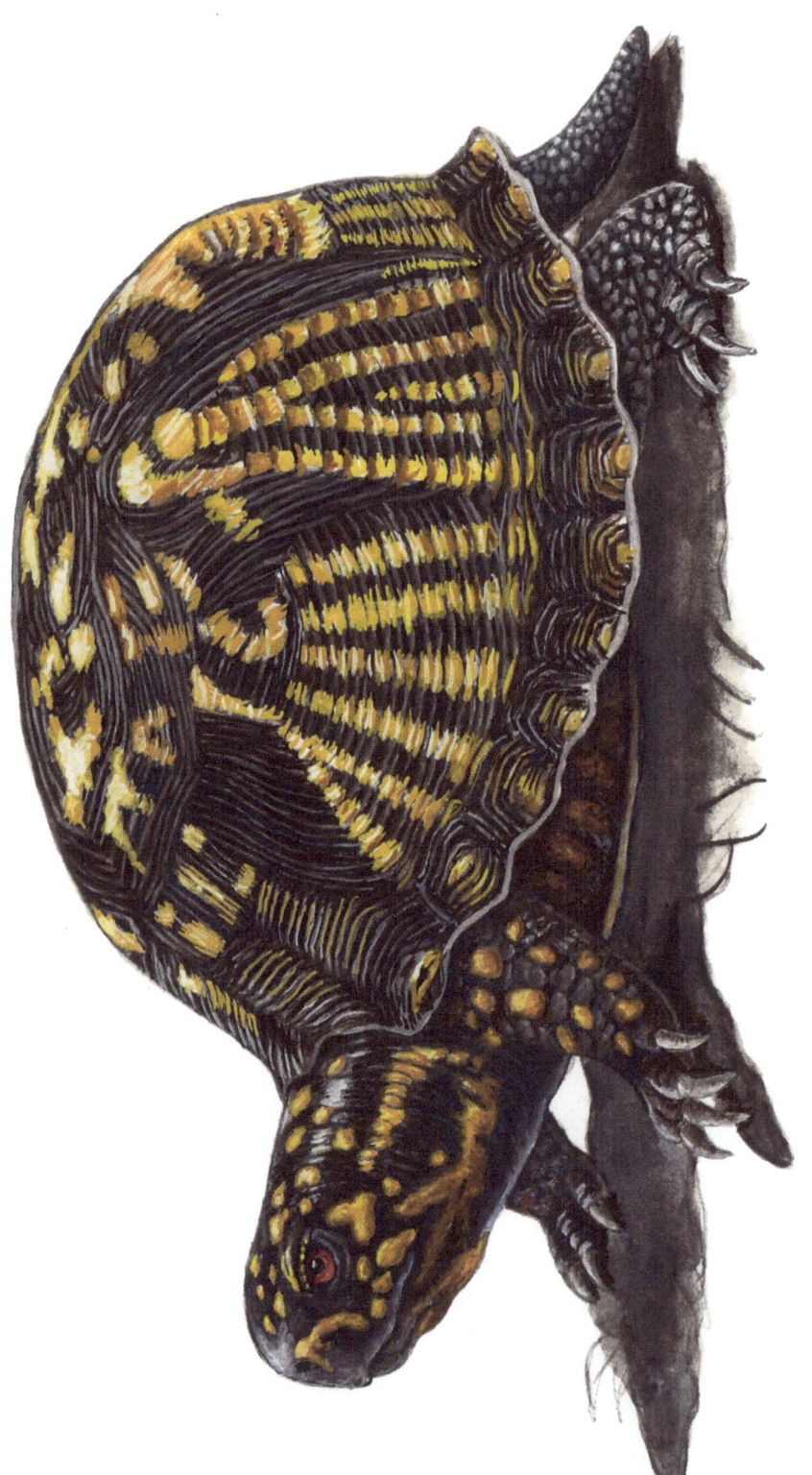

Eastern Box Turtle

Finish *Up!*

(21) With a slightly damp brush, gently blend the edges of the yellow spots into the black of the shell. Blend out the hard edges. Paint in the front edge of the shell with pale gray and blend the edges to soften them. Also, soften all the outside edges of the shell so it doesn't look pasted on the page.

To finish: Put a dark shadow underneath the turtle using a dark mixture of Burnt Umber and Ultramarine Blue. Mix Olive Green with Brilliant Yellow and White and paint a few blades of grass to give your turtle a sense of place.

And you're DONE!

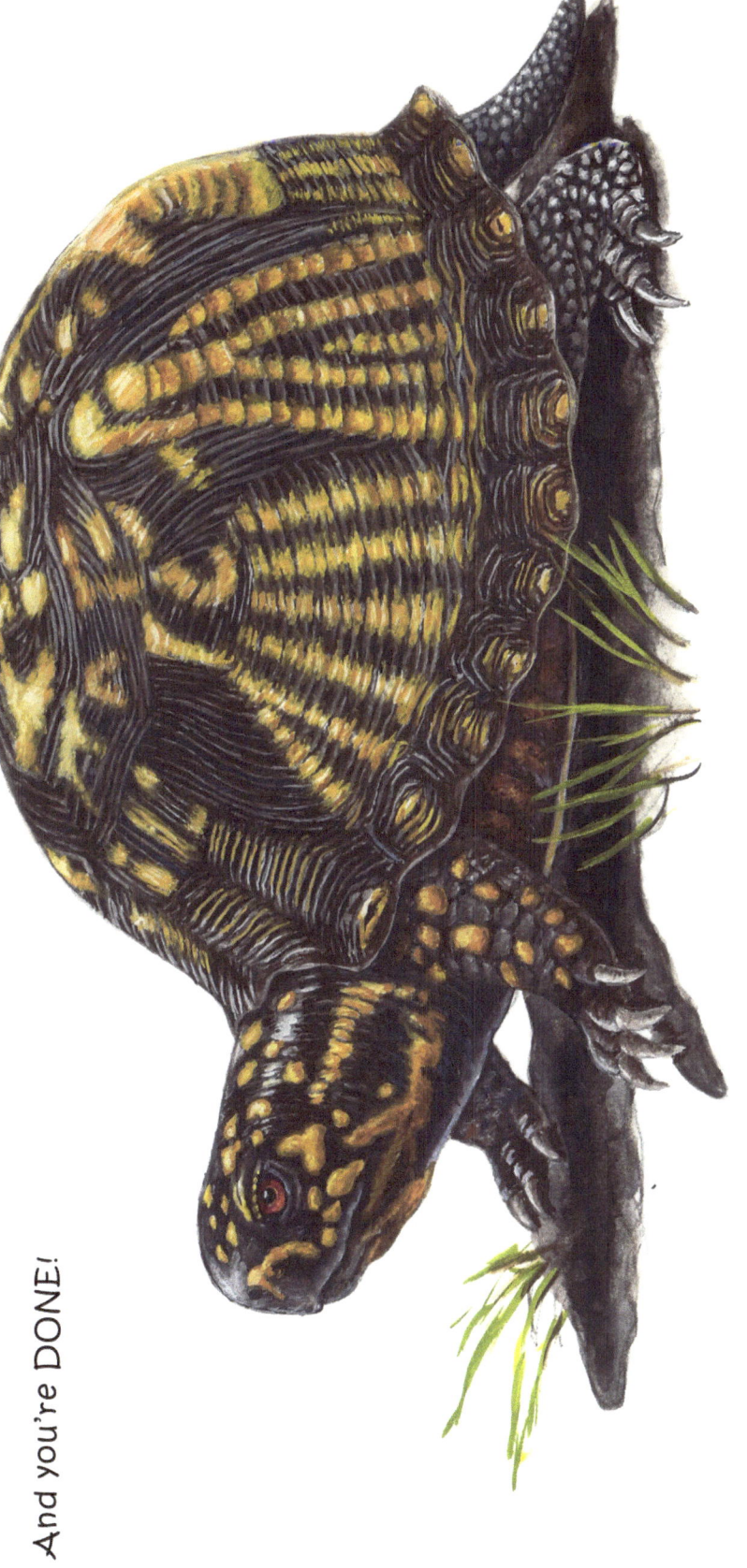

Wrapping Things Up!

Painting glistening eyes, hard shells and bumpy skin is fascinating.
I hope I've inspired you to continue to explore all the possibilities
of using gouache to paint animals. An octogenarian friend of mine,
an accomplished artist, once told me that every time you pick up
a brush it's a learning experience. May you have many!

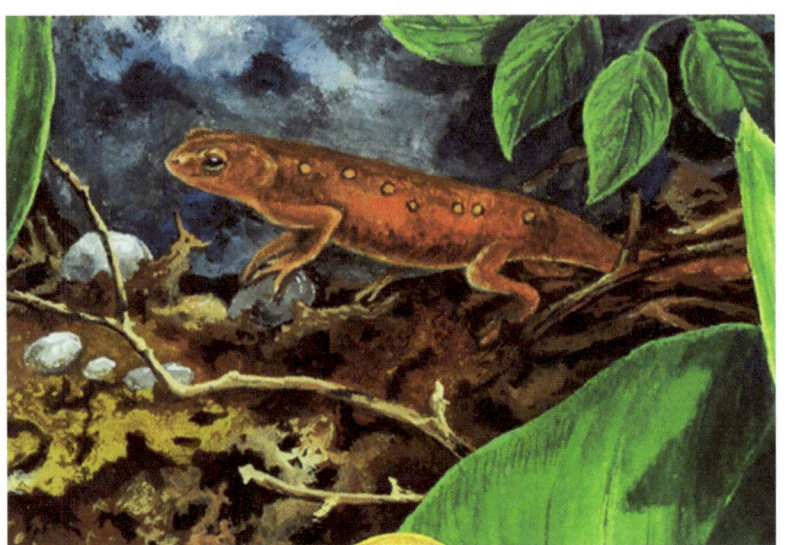

Please check back at Sound of Wings Studio, www.soundofwings.com,
for upcoming courses in gouache!

Currently available:
    Botanical Illustration in Gouache
    Botanical Illustration in Gouache -- the Four Seasons
    Painting Birds in Gouache
    Painting Animals in Gouache
    Painting Butterflies and Moths in Gouache
New for 2015- Composing a Natural Science Illustration

Thanks!

Sandy

Sandy